START WHERE YOU ARE

Retirement Planning in a Changing World

RUTH L. HAYDEN

Kirk House Publishers
Minneapolis, Minnesota

START WHERE YOU ARE
Retirement Planning in a Changing World

by Ruth L. Hayden

Library of Congress Cataloging-In-Publication Data

Hayden, Ruth L., 1946-
  Start where you are : retirement planning in a changing world / Ruth L. Hayden.
      p. cm.
    ISBN 1-886513-65-1 (alk. paper)
      1. Retirement--Planning. I. Title.

HQ1062.H35 2003
646.7'9--dc21

                                                            2003054611

Kirk House Publishers, PO Box 390759, Minneapolis, MN 55439
Manufactured in the United States of America

Acknowledgments

To Leonard Flachman and all the staff at Kirk House Publishers for an efficient and professional publishing process.

To Laura Beaudoin and Gary Legwold, editing.

To Greg and Sally Rademacher, photograph.

To Don for his on-going love and support.

Table of Contents

With love to my

Aunt Leila

and

Aunt Dorothy

who have taught me how to age

with grace and feistiness

Introduction

Dear Reader,

I would like to ask you a personal question, "What do you think your life will be like—20 or 30 years or even 40 years from now— say when you're sixty-five, seventy-five, or ninety?" As a financial educator, I have been asking that question of my clients for more than two decades. If you, like many of my clients, are worried that retirement without financial worry seems less and less like a realistic possibility, this book will help you. In this book, I will show you how to plan for a financially safe retirement—whether the stock market is up (a bull market) or the stock market is down (a bear market), whether you are thirty-two or seventy-two, whether you are male or female, whether you are single or coupled.

"I'll just have to work until I drop dead."

"What's the point? It's not going to be enough money, anyway."

"I just can't think about that right now."

"I'll be able to really get started saving money for retirement when the car gets paid off . . . or when I get that promotion . . . or when the baby gets into full-time school . . . or when our last child is out of college."

"I'll probably just end up a bag lady, anyway."

These, and many more like them, are statements I have heard over the years from clients when I ask them how much money they have invested for retirement or when I ask them what their retirement plans look like.   At best, these statements are unrealistic and worrisome. I explain to my clients that if they want to plan a financially safe retirement they, like you, have to be willing to calculate and plan for retirement differently than they've been taught.   Many people, including some of my clients, believe in the concept of a retirement magic dollar number. In other words, they believe that if they can just save $2 million—or maybe it's $1 million—or maybe it's $800,000—whatever their magic number is—then they can retire and will not have to worry about money ever again.

First and foremost, if you are going to plan a successful retirement, you have to be willing to give up the concept of the magic "worry free" number. This book destroys the myth of the magic number because no one really knows *for sure* how much money it will take to pay for 25 to 35 years of retirement. In those 25 to 35 years the United States will probably experience three, four, or even five bear markets. Some of those bear markets will be long and deep and some will be minor and short-lived. But they will all have a negative effect on that magic number. Unless you're one of about 5 percent of the United States population who has accumulated great wealth, no specific amount of money can guarantee your financial safety for twenty-five or thirty-five years. So instead of the magic number, you can learn a process for managing cash flow that works. This process will help you create financial safety for as long as you live. *Start Where You Are: Retirement Planning in a Changing World* will teach you that process, just like I've taught it to my clients over the past two decades.

In this book you will discover that in planning retirement money is important, very important. But planning the money part of retirement is only about 20 percent of the planning. In fact, 80 percent of planning for a successful retirement is not about money—it's about you! This 80 percent of retirement planning is the self-management part, or as the financial professionals call it, the behavioral science part of money. If you truly want to successfully plan your retirement, 80 percent of that success is determined by how you manage yourself and your emotions.

In *Start Where You Are: Retirement Planning in a Changing World* you will learn how decisions made in fear or greed destroy financial safety. You will learn how to make decisions without these two emotions. And in this book you will learn how to practice the skill of resiliency and the skill of healthy defiance. This book will show you how to view your life in three stages. You will see how these three stages of your life are interconnected and yet how each stage is unique. It will identify for you the three specific time frames within the retirement stage and show you how to successfully plan for each time frame.

Start Where You Are: Retirement Planning in a Changing World will enable you to create a vision statement for retirement and to successfully implement that vision statement.

It will define for you the three facets of retirement planning other than money—the emotional facet, the physical facet, and the spiritual facet. You will learn how to attain balance in these three facets for successful retirement planning.

You will learn about *you*—what is important for you to know about you for retirement planning and what isn't.

You will learn about your *work*—your paid and unpaid work and the role of each in your planning.

You will learn about *money*—proven money principles that will help you build real wealth.

So, again, I ask you, "What do you want your life to be like—say, 30 years from now?"

This book will help you answer that question. And will help you create what it is that you say you want.

Start Where You Are: Retirement Planning in a Changing World provides the information and insight you need to create a life of value and purpose—a life that includes financial safety. So let's get started.

Ruth Hayden

CHAPTER ONE

It's *Never* Too Late!

Not everything that is faced can be changed,
but nothing can be changed until it is faced.
—James Baldwin

Art walked into my office behind his wife, Joan, looking like he'd rather be anywhere but here. After some small talk, I asked Art why he'd come. "My wife made me," he replied. I ignored Joan's deep sigh and asked, "Why do you think Joan wanted you to come?" Art looked at me for a long time and finally said, "Retirement isn't working out exactly as I had planned." Then the story came out.

Art sold his successful contracting business and retired at sixty-five with a significant portfolio—half in the stock market and half in real estate. For two years, until he was sixty-seven, he still had an office in the company and was paid a salary. At age sixty-seven, the salary stopped and his office was assigned to someone else. Art thought he would be pleased with the freedom of not having to go into the office each day, but he forgot that the office was also his social network. He was used to playing golf on Fridays with his friends from work. And he was used to going out to lunches during the week with other people from work. He enjoyed both. When he didn't have an office in the company building, he felt uncomfortable when he went there. So he didn't go anymore. He didn't keep in contact with his work friends. Both the golf and the lunches stopped. When his salary stopped, he didn't realize that his primary hobby also stopped— which, of course, was work. He hadn't thought about how few friends he had outside of work. Art's doctor had just asked him to be evaluated for depression.

In addition, the cash flow wasn't working either. Art had expected to live off of real estate revenue, Social Security, and his wife's professional income, but he was surprised by how much his life cost. He sold some stock investments to pay for the trips he and Joan had been waiting to take.

Art didn't tell his wife.

Joan didn't ask.

He sold more stock to pay for the cash flow shortfall each month. This shortfall was exacerbated by Joan's new part-time status at work. Joan had been recently diagnosed with multiple sclerosis and needed to significantly reduce her work hours to have the time to take care of herself.

Then Art and Joan sold their house and paid significantly more for their new home than they expected. Again Art sold investments to make up the difference. This time, though, he also sold a significant real estate investment.

Again he didn't tell his wife.

Again, she didn't ask.

Now at the age of seventy-three, only six years into his full retirement, in good health, with his total portfolio already depleted by half, Art was feeling both a little desperate and a little defensive. Joan was scared and angry, and she made it clear that their marriage was vulnerable.

This was the situation that brought Art and Joan to my office. Both were clear that this wasn't the way they thought their lives would be in retirement.

So what happened? Why didn't Art's retirement planning work?

It's really quite simple. Art's retirement planning didn't work because he was working under the old model of retirement. The old model works like this:

Ah-h-h-h! Retirement! The daily grind is finally over. Dealing with office politics, the rush-hour traffic, and the exhaustion—it's over. It's time to travel a bit, get the workbench and closets organized, hit the golf course, start reading that stack of books, see the grandkids. Ah-h-h-h! And then? Death.

The old model of retirement says that retirement is supposed to be like an extended vacation. You work hard—very hard—until you reach the magical age we call retirement. Then it's reward time! You have the money and the time to do all the things you've been waiting years to do. You feel happy and satisfied.

The Finish-Line Model of Retirement Is Outdated Because of Projected Longevity

This socially accepted model of retirement is called the *finish-line model.* You ran the race, you did well, and now it's reward time. This old model of retirement was Art's model. It might have been valid because, based on male longevity in his family, Art should already be dead. That's the plain truth. Instead he is desperate and defensive.

But the good and bad news is that Art isn't dead. He is alive and well, and worried.

The finish-line model of retirement is outdated because projected lifespans are longer. Some people recognize this, but instead of creating an entirely new model, they simply rework the old model. Their reworking of the old model looks like this:

Ah-h-h-h! Retirement! The daily grind is finally over. Dealing with office politics, the rush-hour traffic, and the exhaustion—it's over. It's time to travel a bit, get the workbench and closets organized, hit the golf course, start reading that stack of books, see the grandkids. Ah-h-h-h! And then? Twenty and more years of the same.

As you can see, the reworked model looks the same, except now the expectation is that we'll live longer. Neither the old finish-line retirement model nor the reworked retirement model is satisfactory. When the Social Security system was established in 1935, people lived, on the average, to the ripe old age of sixty-two. Most people died before they actually were able to receive their Social Security benefits. In other words, they never reached the finish line.

In the 1950s the average retirement age was sixty-seven and the average life expectancy was seventy-one. Through the 50s and 60s the finish-line model of retirement worked. Think about it. The model was successful because most workers (primarily men) actually reached the finish line—they had time for a little travel, finished house projects, played a little golf, and died before they got bored (or their wives did), *and* before they ran out of money. They ran the race. They did well. Then came reward time—for four to five years.

The finish-line model of retirement is hard to give up because the people who role-modeled this for you were so positive about it. Those four or five years looked really good to them. This retirement model seemed to work for that generation—particularly for men.

But statistics tell us that the finish-line model didn't work quite so well for women. Men died early enough so they didn't run out of money, but many times the men's pensions died with them. Eighty percent of women in retirement back then—as well as 80 percent of women today—didn't have pension plans in their own names. The result, then and now, was financially vulnerable women. Women were and are vulnerable in part because they live longer than men. Studies show that women receive significantly less in monthly Social Security income than men, not only because they earn less than men but also because they are in the work force about eleven years less than men. And, finally, women didn't—and still don't—invest enough money for their own retirements. (Retirement investing will be covered in chapter 9.)

What You Learned About Retirement You Learned from Role Models

You've learned what retirement *should* be like from watching your role models plan for and live through retirement. These role models might be your parents or your grandparents. Your most profound learning was probably from watching and listening to your same-sex role models. If you're a man, that would be your father or grandfather. If you're a woman, your mother or your grandmother is a primary role model. Aunts, uncles, religious leaders, and teachers also serve as models.

Think about what you learned from these adults. What did you see, hear, and observe about what retirement is *supposed* to be like? Take time to think about the following questions:

Who was your primary adult, same–sex role model for retirement?

What age was "old" to your primary, same-sex role model?

Was retirement something this person looked forward to?

Did you hear this person planning for retirement?

What kind of planning did you see? Was the planning full of anticipation? Was the planning full of worry?

When retirement actually did occur, what happened?

Did the retirement years seem to be successful? Did you see contentment? Did you see worry? Did you see frustration? What else did you see?

How long has retirement lasted for each of your role models?

Now, based on what you observed, what have you learned about retirement from your role models? (By the way, don't think about whether you like what you learned. Just simply ask yourself what you learned based on your observations.)

Whatever your answers, there are several reasons the finish-line model of retirement probably will not work for you.

First, this model doesn't take into account increased longevity for both men and women. Most of your role models ran a much shorter race than you will. In other words, most of you will live longer than your role models. This longevity makes it necessary that you change how you plan your life.

Another reason this finish-line model doesn't work is that women have changed. One of the ways women have changed is that more women are divorced, which increases their financial vulnerability. A divorced woman's net worth is almost 40 percent less than that of a woman who never married. Partly because of this reduced net worth, most women will not be able to retire at sixty-two or sixty-five—the age that they "should" be able to retire according to the finish-line model of retirement— because they will not have enough money without their work income.

The finish-line model doesn't work for men either, because men also have changed. Most men aren't willing—anymore—to stay in a job they don't like just to have a good retirement, even if it were possible. Men expect their jobs to pay them a good salary so they can have a good life. They also expect their jobs to be rewarding—allowing them to advance their skills and their status. These expectations are in addition to being able to accumulate money through their jobs for their retirement years.

And finally, both men *and* women expect a higher quality of life than most of their parents and grandparents thought was possible. They want more choices. They want to be more comfortable. They want to do more things. They want to see more places.

For the generation or two before this one, the last years of retirement often looked harsher, more frugal, and more fearful than most are willing to accept. I remember listening to the fear of my paternal grandmother as she worried about being alone. She also worried about falling, about how she was going to pay for her next prescription, and about how she was going to re-place her glasses which didn't work so well anymore. I remember watching her live in semi-darkness because she worried about the electric bill. I remember her crying. I remember vowing that my life would be different. I remember wishing I were older so I could help.

Think for a moment about your role models. What have you learned about retirement from them that you don't want for yourself in your own retirement?

Most of you—both men and women—expect more than what you saw your role models experience, much more. You want more choices, and better choices, with more fun, for longer. Increased longevity is *good news*.

The outdated and ineffective finish-line model needs to be discarded—not simply reworked. If you want your life to work, you need a new model for retirement. This book provides the tools to help you develop that model.

It doesn't matter what your age—**start where you are**. Start to plan for the rest of your life.

CHAPTER TWO

Life Is a Series of Stages

*It takes a deep commitment to change
and an even deeper commitment to grow.
—Ralph Ellison*

Sometimes I wish we could simply get rid of the word *retirement* altogether. As long as we still use that word, we will have a tendency to try to make retirement be the same thing it was for the generations before us. We will continue to work and rework the old finish-line model—to no avail. Reworking the old model is ineffective and discouraging. This old model makes increased longevity seem like bad news! This old model of retirement makes no allowance for living—living long and well.

Increased longevity is the reality. Living long needs to be good news for you, not bad news. You need a brand new definition of the word retirement—a new model of retirement that reflects your new longevity and helps you live well. You need a model that gives you a useable road map for life—all of life.

It's more productive and accurate to think of your retirement as simply one of life's developmental stages—no more and no less. When you view your life in three primary stages, retirement is simply the third and final stage of your life. Stage one is birth to thirty years old. Stage two is thirty to sixty years old. Stage three is sixty to ninety years and beyond.

It is important that you understand this concept of three developmental stages. Therefore, we will explore how each stage is unique and what each stage needs to make it work. And, even more importantly, you must understand how interrelated these three stages really are—how the planning of one stage directly impacts the success of the next stage.

So, first, it's important to understand the uniqueness of each stage. To do this, let's reminisce a little as you travel back to the first stage of your life. Based on your present age, it may be a long trip or a short trip. But, with a little nostalgia, travel back to your first developmental stage.

Developmental Stage One: Birth to Age Thirty

Birth to adolescence to college to a first career is a developmental stage. This first stage of your life represents about one-third of your life. Stage one is about learning to walk and talk. It's about diapers and potty training. It's about rebellion and acne. It's about a first kiss, cramming for tests, moving away from home, job interviews, and learning how much of your earned money goes to pay income taxes. Remember? These events are all part of the uniqueness of the first stage.

From your own unique experience and in your own words, how would you describe some of the events in the first third of your life? Take a moment. Reminisce a little.

Do you remember your first day of kindergarten?

Do you remember your first high school football game?

Who was your favorite teacher in high school?

What was your favorite date? What did you do?

How was your first night in the college dorm?

What was your first job? Did you like it?

Do you remember the first book you read? What was it?

What was the first pet you had? What happened to that pet?

Do you remember your first paycheck? Did it seem like a lot of money or not so much?

A lot happened in this first developmental stage of your life. Feeling enormous hope for the future while dealing with the fear of the unknown are two of the conflicting emotions present in the first third of your life.

Do you remember the hopes and fears of the first stage of your life?

What other emotions were/are part of your first stage of life?

What caused/causes these emotions?

How did/do you show these emotions in this first stage of your life?

In the latter part of stage one, most individuals give a lot of thought to what will happen in the next stage—stage two, which lasts from ages thirty to sixty. Most people are full of plans about all the accomplishments they expect to experience in stage two. During stage one very little thought is given to stage three, which encompasses the "retirement" years—ages sixty to ninety and beyond. Most people don't want to think about getting old because they believe the accomplishment time of their lives will be over and done by then. The only connection that most people in stage one have to stage three is that in their twenties they may be contributing money to a retirement plan of some kind. Otherwise, stage three is pretty much a non-issue. Stage three seems far away, a time of old age.

Developmental Stage Two: Ages Thirty to Sixty

The middle third of life is the second developmental stage. The uniqueness of this stage may involve settling into a first home, establishing a family, and building a successful work life. It's about diapers and day care. It's about office politics and expensive parking. It's about learning how to put grout around your bathtub and learning the value of gutters on the house. It's about getting less sleep than you ever thought possible except the time you took that final exam in college after an all-night party. It's about rent versus home equity.

As in stage one, this 30-year period is multidimensional—it's a long time with a lot of living, a lot of events, and a lot of changes. As this stage continues, it's also about aging parents, empty nests, and glass ceilings. It's about putting money for retirement in mutual funds and watching the money grow; it's about putting money in mutual funds and watching the money shrink. It's about bills and more bills but never feeling like you're getting ahead. And it's about work and more work—or did I already mention that?

From your own perspective and experiences, how would you describe some of the unique events in the second stage of your life—ages thirty to sixty?

Emotionally, this second stage is about excitement, exhaustion, accomplishment, and frustration. It's about learning where you have control in your life and where you don't. It's about incredible joy and incredible disillusionment. It's about unmet expectations and hope.

Were/are any of these emotions part of the second stage of development for you?

What other emotions were/are part of your second stage of life?

What caused/causes these emotions?

How did/do you show these emotions in stage two of your life?

To most people in stage two, financial accumulation for stage three is an important goal. That doesn't mean they're actually putting away enough money for stage three, but they still have the goal. The daily busyness of stage two uses both time and money far faster than most people could have predicted. The reality of the needs of today takes precedence for most people in stage two over the future needs of stage three. Stage three still seems far away, except for those times when they look in the mirror and see new lines and new gray hairs. Then stage three doesn't seem so far away.

During stage two you wonder how you will make stage three work. And, sometimes, you worry.

Developmental Stage Three: Ages Sixty to Ninety—and Beyond

The final third of life is what we usually have referred to as retirement. Stage three may be the same length of time as the other two stages—maybe even longer. This stage is also multidimensional, like stages one and two. Stage three is about more free time, less money, less energy, and having more choice regarding the use of time. It's about traveling and reading and gardening and golf. It's about memories. It's about aching bones and sleeplessness. At the same time, it's about feeling increased vitality because of fewer responsibilities. It's about a new awareness of the preciousness of time and one's own mortality. In this stage there are usually fewer demands from the outside world and more demands from one's body.

Life in this stage is about the pleasure of grandchildren and the pleasure of volunteering. It's about cleaning the counter in the kitchen and it staying clean. It's about leaving the newspaper on the table and it staying there. It's about order. It's about loneliness. It's about the joy of long-time friends. It's about the pain of saying good-bye to those friends. It's about worry when the value of investments decrease. It's about having the time to learn another language and the pleasure of realizing the brain is still sharp. It's about patience.

From your perspective—through your own experiences or by watching your parents and grandparents—how would you describe stage three?

How long do you think stage three will last for you? In other words, how long do you think you will live?

Why do you think you will live that long? Is this length of time pleasant to think about or worrisome to think about?

Stage three brings a sense of freedom in the moment and worry about the future at the same time.

What emotions do you experience or do you think you'll experience as part of the third stage of development?

What circumstances cause or will cause these emotions?

How will you show or how do you think you will show these emotions in stage three of your life?

All Stages Are Interrelated

All three stages of life are interrelated, of course. What you do or don't do in one stage will directly affect the success of your life in the next stage.

If you want to have your teeth when you're seventy years old—in stage three—you'll need to see a dentist in stages one and two.

If you want to buy a house when you're thirty years old—in stage two—you can't ruin your credit with a bankruptcy when you're twenty-eight—in stage one.

If you want money to pay the bills in your retirement—in stage three—you'll need to figure out what a 401(k), or 403(b), or SEP-IRA really is *and* actually put money into it—in stages one and two.

If you don't want your heart to quit on you when you're sixty-eight—in stage three—you'll want to quit smoking in stage one.

If you want a healthy love partnership when you're thirty-five—stage two—you'll want to begin to develop your healthy self in stage one so you have the capacity to love and be a good partner. Or if you wait until stage two, it may take you until late stage two or early stage three before you can do your part to make a healthy relationship work.

If you want your brain to work when you're seventy-five—stage three—you'll need to think and think again and keep thinking in stage two.

If you acquire $50,000 in student debt in stage one, you'll have fewer choices in your lifestyle in stage two and won't be able to invest as much for stage three.

If you want your kids to *want* to visit you when you're seventy—stage three—you'd better be a vital part of their lives in stage two.

If you don't want to live with regrets when you're eighty—stage three—you'd better take the time to figure out your values and the meaning of life during stage two.

All three stages are interrelated. What you do in one stage directly affects the choices you have in the next stage. If your life is going to work in stage three—retirement—you need to purposefully plan your life to work in *all* three interrelated stages.

Before you can develop a workable strategy for planning in each of the three stages of your life, including the third stage, you'll want to prepare yourself by learning crucial life-planning and self-management skills. The next four chapters will help you learn these essential life-planning skills. If you don't have these skills, you will not be successful in developing or, even more importantly, following your life-plan.

CHAPTER THREE

Avoiding Second Arrows

They control their destiny because they control themselves.
—*George Samuel Clason,* The Richest Man in Babylon *(1926)*

Several years ago, when my family went through what my grandmother would call a "rough patch," I said to my doctor, "If someone comes in and tells you how well her life is working all of a sudden—and she tells you that, surprisingly, her life used to be miserable and now it's good—I want you to know that for some reason that person got my life, and I want it back." I told my doctor that my life had been going along fine and then everything fell apart. I just couldn't understand it. "How could so much go so wrong in such a short time?" I asked him. "Nothing is happening the way I thought it would." My doctor looked at me sympathetically and said that he understood. Actually, he felt the same way about his life. He told me he hadn't planned on a recent divorce. And he was still trying to figure out how to put his life back together again. My doctor and I commiserated about how unpredictable and discouraging life sometimes can be.

In my office, on a daily basis, I hear words from frustrated, discouraged clients. I hear, "You don't understand, Ruth. This is not the way I thought my life would be. This is not what I thought would happen. What am I supposed to do now? It's not fair!"

Or, as one man said to me, "Someone changed all the rules, and no one gave me a vote! It's not right!"

Those words are said with a sense of helpless frustration—of anger, of discouragement, of hopeless confusion.

A client could be talking about a relationship change: "It's not fair, Ruth," Katherine told me in my office one afternoon. "I worked nights as a nurse to put that man through law school. I worked overtime when he was trying to build his practice. We have three beautiful children—two are in college. It's finally my turn. I'm back in school and loving it. And guess what? He's decided to have an affair with another lawyer—who is also married. Our marriage is over. The kids are devastated, and I'm angry and scared. It really isn't fair!"

Or a client could be talking about a health problem: He sat in front of me—absolutely rigid. Ray and I had worked together for almost two years now. Over two years ago, Ray had been laid off from his job and had decided to use that opportunity to start his own business—the one he had always wanted and knew he could do. And it worked. He developed a product and a brand. He had more business than he and a full-time secretary could handle and was considering a step that would significantly grow his business.

"What did the doctor say?" I asked him.

"Prostate cancer," Ray replied. "I will need surgery and radiation treatments. I can't believe the timing of this. Everything was going so well, and now this. It's devastating."

Or the client could be talking about a job layoff: "Well, I guess the whole family is in jeopardy," John explained to me. "With me being laid off, I don't know how we'll even be able to afford to continue the health care for the baby. It's not right, Ruth. My production was the highest it's ever been, and I got laid off. I don't understand. It doesn't do any good to work hard and produce. No one is loyal anymore."

Or it could be a loss of retirement investments: "My greatest nightmare," Leigh explained after showing me his latest portfolio summary, "is that I'll have to be a Wal-Mart greeter when I'm eighty."

There are so many ways a person can feel out of control and confused.

Ask yourself:

Have I, like so many others, ever felt as if life has given me an unfair challenge? A bad break?

What happened?

How did it feel to have that happen?

How did I respond?

My Life Hasn't Turned Out the Way I Thought It Would

I know that every one of my clients has one thing—and probably only one thing—in common. Some circumstance in their lives didn't turn out exactly as they thought it would. Sometimes life turns out better than they expected, but more often than not, they feel that something has turned out much worse. I know this is true for all my clients because if their lives had turned out exactly as they thought they would, they wouldn't have made an appointment with me. They would be going on their merry way—everything predictable and happy.

But that, of course, isn't life.

When life doesn't work the way you thought it would, it takes courage to keep going. It takes courage to step out of the helplessness and hopelessness of disappointment. It takes courage to move forward with plans when you are angry and frustrated. It takes courage to move out of powerlessness and into action—when you don't have the confidence that it will do any good anyway. It takes courage to begin planning your life again.

When something difficult and disappointing happens, two possible consequences come out of the difficulty:

The first consequence is the difficulty itself. You must be willing to face the challenge of figuring out how to actually get through the difficulty—whether it is an illness, a relationship change, or a job layoff. You must ask yourself, "Now what am I going to do?" And you must be able to find the courage to do it.

The second consequence when something difficult and disappointing happens in your life is your own emotional response. Some people get stuck in their own emotional mire. This emotional mire is the single biggest reason that individuals aren't able to move forward—that they're not able to form and carry out their life-plan. This emotional mire isn't the difficulty that happened to you—stuff happens to everyone! This mire is your own emotional response to the difficulty. It is what you say to yourself when something bad happens in your life. It is the way you respond when life doesn't go the way you thought it would.

Bad things happen to everyone. But the second bad thing that can happen to you is what you *do* to yourself—what you *say* to yourself. Sophocles said, "The greatest griefs are those we cause ourselves." In Buddhism, these griefs we cause ourselves are called the second arrow. The first arrow can hurt you. Everyone experiences first arrows; everyone goes through times that produce pain. But it's the second arrow that can truly stop you. The second arrow can kill your spirit. It can kill your life-planning. Remember, you and you alone have control over whether this second arrow—your emotional response to the difficulty—will strike you.

Emotional second arrows are expressed in many ways:

"I give up—my portfolio is down by almost 50 percent. I'll never be able to quit work. It's not fair. What's the point anyway? Might as well spend the money now and have some fun."

"Why even try? Nothing really matters, anyway."

Or:

"I'm so discouraged. I just want to quit. Can a person just quit when it's too hard and no fun anymore?"

"Everyone else seems to be able to plan for retirement. I'm just not good enough with money."

"Something else always needs my time or my money—I never have anything left for me, for my life."

Or:

"No one seems to care anyway."

"I'll never earn enough money."

"I'll never pick the right places to invest my money anyway."

"It doesn't do any good to work hard and be productive."

Do you hear the helpless, hopeless frustration?

Earlier in this chapter you identified a personal experience that you felt was unfair—that was a hardship or a bad break for you. What did you identify?

Now ask yourself:

What did I say to myself when I experienced that life difficulty?

Did what I said to myself help me or hurt me? Did it encourage me to move on or did that language stop me and make me stuck for a while?

If what you said to yourself stopped you—got you stuck in your own emotional mire—that was your second arrow.

When I hear this second arrow language in my clients, at first, just for a moment, I sympathize with the person. But just for a moment. Then the teacher part of me steps in and says, "You need to stop hurting yourself. Yes, what happened to you is very difficult. But now you're hurting yourself. You deserve better. You can decide to stop hurting yourself."

Then I say, "Come on! You can make your life work if you want to. You don't have to get stuck. This problem is solvable. I will help you."

What I just role-modeled for my clients and for you is what I call healthy defiance. It's that feisty, four-year-old in you who wants to say, "I can *so* do it if I want! Watch me!"

It's healthy defiance that says, "No second arrow for me! I know I'm discouraged and confused right now, but I'll figure this out. For goodness' sake, I have to figure this out. It's my life. My life has to work—whether I'm twenty-four years old or sixty-five years old."

If you can control your emotions, you can control your life. If you can manage your mind and control what you say to yourself, you can make this life-planning book actually work for you. This doesn't mean difficulties won't arise. And this doesn't mean you won't be disappointed—whether with your partner, the stock market, or your aching back. But this *does* mean that you'll be able to express your discouragement and then turn from the second arrow by moving forward into that healthy, defiant part of you that asks, "What do I need to do right now to make my life work? My life has to work!"

Deciding to take control of your emotions is the first step in preparing yourself to make your life-planning really work. It enables you to focus on the solutions rather than being overwhelmed by the problem.

CHAPTER FOUR

What If . . . Then What?

Only I can change my life. No one can do it for me.
—Carol Burnett

A couple of years ago, I was sitting and talking with an elderly aunt. I can't tell you her age, because she considers age to be a private matter. I asked my aunt to tell me, based on her experience, how a person ages with some degree of satisfaction. I wanted to know what people needed to know to make their lives work—and work well. After some thought, she said, "There are so many ways to answer that question, Ruth. But, I could mention a few things that I believe contribute to a positive aging process. First, you have to have money so you can take care of yourself or be able to pay for the care you need. You need more money than you think you do. Pretend that you are going to live much longer than you ever thought you would and that you will need to pay for more help than you ever thought you would. Make sure you have that kind of money. Money gives you choices. When you have choices, you don't feel as trapped by a deteriorating body." (We'll work more specifically with money in chapter 9.)

"Also," she continued, "as we get older, all of us—men and women—need to feel that we are useful to someone, somehow, in some capacity. This conversation is an example of usefulness,

Ruth, because you're asking for my advice. And that feels good. Usefulness can also be work—paid or voluntary work. It doesn't matter. But in some way, someone, somewhere needs to need me. If you don't have this, what's the point? There's no joy or satisfaction in being a burden. One has to—absolutely has to—feel useful." (We'll work more specifically with the concept of useful work in chapter 8.)

"And finally," my aunt said, "you have to be enormously resilient and flexible. If you stay stuck in how you thought life was supposed to be, you'll never make it. What most people don't understand is that you have to practice being resilient before you get old like me. If you wait until you are old, it's too late, because you're already set in your ways. It's too difficult. You can't be a beginner at being resilient when you are facing major life changes—and they can happen throughout life, but it seems there are more major life changes when one is old. And they seem to come faster. I also believe you have to have a spiritual belief that there is a reason for your life—that your life has a purpose. That somehow all of the events in your life are connected and work together. I think of my life as a patchwork quilt. Until I die, I just keep adding pieces. Somehow, in a way that I can't see right now, the quilt will all come together and be beautiful. This spiritual belief really helps, I believe, in learning to be resilient."

My aunt went on to explain. "When I lost my husband a couple of years ago, as much as I grieved for him, there was another part of me that knew I could make it. I had always made it. And I would again. That's faith and practiced resiliency. When I had to move out of my home, it was so very difficult. I was angry and scared—but I also knew that I would adjust, because I always had. Do you see what I mean? You have to know how to be flexible—to adjust and to know you will find a way to make your life work. And you have to know you can do this before the really big tests come. You have to practice resiliency now, Ruth. You have to see resiliency as something you have to master if you want to have a long and satisfying life."

This wonderful, aging role model is absolutely right, you know. Resiliency is a skill that must be practiced. All of us have to let go of our emotional rigidity about how we thought life was *supposed* to be or what we *thought* would happen. In chapter 3, you learned to get out of your own way. You learned to avoid the "second arrow." You learned that bad things happen and that your emotional response can make your life better or it can make it worse, depending upon how you respond. You learned that to make your life-planning work, you need to learn the skill of managing your emotions so you don't get stuck in your own emotional mire.

But to make the life-planning strategies—presented in this book—actually work, you need to teach yourself another new skill. That is the skill of estimating and predicting. I call it the skill of *resiliency.*

Remember putting together puzzles as a child? You would pick up a piece and look at it, then look at the board with the puzzle pieces that were already in place. To find a space for that little piece you asked yourself, "What if I put it here? Then what will happen? Will it fit? Will I need to look for a different space? I won't know until I try." And so you kept trying to find a space where your puzzle piece would fit. You kept strategizing each little piece—sometimes you were right the first time and sometimes it took several tries to find the right space. Sometimes you gave up, put the piece down, and went on to another piece.

Life is like a puzzle. My aunt called it a patchwork quilt. You plan and plan—sometimes your plan works and sometimes, because of new circumstances, it doesn't. But you never quit. That's resiliency. You can't quit. You can't just say, "Forget this puzzle. It's too hard. It's not worth it. It won't do any good anyway. I'll never figure out how to make this thing work!" You can't say that because we aren't talking about a simple puzzle. We're talking about your life. It is your life, and you have to make your life right for you. You have to be willing to keep trying to make your life work. Those who have mastered resiliency say,

"Okay, so that didn't work. Now what am I going to do? What are my options?"

As you go through your life, you will need to purposefully practice the skill of resiliency. Learning to be resilient means that you are constantly asking yourself two questions.

The first question explores the options: "What if I did this? What if I said this? What if I saved this much per month? What if I wrote my resumé this way? What if I volunteered at this organization? What if I bought this townhouse? What if . . . ? What if . . . ? What if . . . ?"

The second question explores the results: "Then what will happen? Will I get the job? Will I be saving enough? Will I be able to help and feel satisfaction? Will I like living there? Then what . . . ? Then what . . . ? Then what . . . ?"

When you use these two question techniques to figure out the puzzle pieces of your life, you are practicing the skill of resiliency—the skill of estimating and predicting your actions. This skill is absolutely necessary for successful life-planning.

"All right, Ruth," my client Leigh said with a sigh. "So just because my portfolio is way down, it doesn't mean my only choice is to be a Wal-Mart greeter. Which, of course, scares me to death. You're saying I need to move on and quit obsessing about the market and its impact on my future. Right? You're saying I need to start figuring out what else could work and get moving. Do I hear you correctly, Ruth?"

"Absolutely," I told Leigh. "If you can't be more resilient now when you have so many possible choices and many years to make things happen, what are you going to do when you're old and bad things happen? What can you do to move on and try something different so you can make your life work?" I asked.

"Well," Leigh asked thoughtfully, "*what if* I increased my contribution to my 401(k) by 5 percent—that would put me at 12 percent? I need to check with my accountant to see how much I would actually lose in my net pay. *Then* Denise and I will have to rework our budget to see if the cash flow can work. Then if that works and we can continue to pay all our bills, *what if*, in six months, I increased my contribution another 3 percent, *then,* I wonder if I can accumulate enough money? *What if* I did this until sixty-eight rather than sixty-five? *Then* maybe I'd really have enough money. What do you think, Ruth?"

"I think it's a good start," I told Leigh. "I think you're beginning to practice the skill of resiliency quite well. Keep figuring it out. Keep practicing."

Remember Katherine who had just started back in school when she found out her husband was having an affair? The divorce was almost final the day she sat in my office and exclaimed, "It's all so hopeless! I don't know how I can begin to figure out my life and what to do next. Since he left me for that other woman, I feel old and stuck. I have no idea where to start."

"I know you feel your life has been devastated by this," I said to Katherine very calmly. "And I also have every confidence that you can put it back together again. I know you can learn to deal with your anger and hopelessness and figure out what you will do next." Then I reminded her, "Remember, if you can manage your emotions, you can manage your life. And," I continued, quite emphatically, "you really don't have a choice. You have to get on with your life! I know you have the skill of resiliency because you are raising children. As a successful parent, you have learned to adjust and move on when your children surprised you with their own life-planning scenarios."

"I know what you mean," Katherine interjected with a laugh. "My kids have taught me to be enormously resilient by giving me many challenges. So now I have to practice that resiliency in my own life, and I have to teach them resiliency, too, so they can move on after this divorce."

"You've got it, Katherine," I said. "So what are you going to do first to practice this skill?"

"*What if,*" Katherine began, "I checked at the school to see if they have any internships—and what they'd pay or if they would give reduced tuition? *Then,* I wonder if I could continue in school?"

"What if," I asked, "you scheduled a meeting with a career counselor to find out what you'd be really good at and what would give you enough income to provide a good life for you? *Then,* would you need to change your major? *Then,* how would your financial future look?"

"Good idea," Katherine replied. "As hard as this is going to be, it actually feels better to be practicing options rather than just feeling hopeless. This feels so much more hopeful."

When your life doesn't work out the way you thought it would, you already know from reading chapter 4 that it takes courage to keep moving forward, not stuck in fear. You have to manage your emotions. But now you're learning that you also have to develop the skill of estimating and predicting. Being resilient means you won't get stuck because you don't know what to do. Learning to be resilient means you'll develop confidence about your competency to make your life work. When life doesn't go the way you planned, you know you'll find another solution, another plan—because you always have.

Where in my life am I a little stuck right now? A little discouraged? Where haven't my plans worked the way I thought they would?

How can you find ways to practice the skill of resiliency in this area you just identified? Ask yourself:

What if I . . . ?

***Then* what do I think could happen?**

Then ask yourself again:

If that doesn't work, what if I . . . ?

***Then* what do I think could happen?**

Keep practicing.

What if . . . ? Then what?

What if . . . ? Then what?

Resiliency is a skill that requires daily practice. Every day, look for ways to practice this skill: *What if I did it this way? Then what do I think will happen?*

These two little questions will help you find solutions when you think there are none. These two questions will teach you the life-planning skill of resiliency that is essential for success in all three stages of life.

CHAPTER FIVE

My Life Has to Work—All of It!

Change your thoughts and you change your world.
—Norman Vincent Peale

The other day I ran into my friend Adam at a coffee shop. "How are you, Adam?" I asked as I gave him a hug.

"Actually, Ruth, I've never been worse."

"Is everything all right with Betsy?" I asked.

"Oh, Betsy's fine," said Adam. "We just celebrated our 23rd wedding anniversary."

"So what's wrong?" I persisted.

"Sometimes I wonder what the point of all of this really is," Adam said despondently.

"It's the kids, isn't it?" I asked.

"The kids are fine. Sarah is going off to college in a few weeks. And the other two are still in high school."

Now I was feeling frustrated. I felt like I was playing the game of Twenty Questions and I still didn't have a clue. "Adam, what's wrong? Is it your health?"

"No, it's not my health," he responded. "I simply don't know what to do. My retirement portfolio is down by about 40 percent. I can't figure it out."

At first Adam had sounded dejected, but now he sounded angry. "I'm about to fire my financial planner for screwing up my investments so badly. I know the guy is an old family friend, but I can't believe I paid him to lose money for me. I think he's a crook." Then Adam continued very sadly, "I don't think I'll ever be able to retire. I'll just have to work until I drop dead."

"Adam," I interrupted, "you're only forty-four years old. What's the matter with you? Your marriage is good, your kids are good, your health is good, and I assume work is good. And you're calling a family friend a 'crook'? You have time to rebuild your portfolio and, even if you didn't, life is still good. For goodness' sake, Adam, get a grip!"

Life is not all about money! It may seem strange for a financial consultant to say this, but it's absolutely true. Money is important, but it's only one measure of the success of your life. And it's only one measure of the success of your life-planning for retirement.

In preparing yourself to life-plan for retirement, which is what this book is about, you have to understand that the planning has to include much more than money. Oh, it has to include money, absolutely! Without money it is difficult to plan everything else. But what you and my friend Adam have to remember is that even with money for your retirement, not much else may work either. The goal of life-planning for retirement—and the goal of this book—is to get *all* facets of your life working and in balance, including money.

In order for life-planning to work at its optimal level, you need to consider four independent yet interrelated facets of life-planning: spiritual life, emotional life, physical life, and financial life.

What's the point of having a lot of money if your heart quits on you? What's the point of having a healthy heart if you don't have the money to pay for the roof over your head? What's the point of having a great brain and being a whiz at crossword puzzles if you're depressed and living with regret because nothing in your life seems to matter?

Spiritually, emotionally, physically, and financially—working with these four facets is an integrated approach to life-planning.

A balance of these four facets is essential for successful life-planning.

My Spiritual Life: Why Am I Here?

Why are you here anyway? Why are you working at the daily grind day after day? What's the point of it all? When you're at the end of your life, what about your life will hold true meaning? I define *spiritual* as life purpose. It can also be defined as connection to a higher power. Spiritual can be defined as living according to your core values. For most people to have a balanced life both now and in retirement, they have to feel connected to something bigger than simply the day's schedule or what's happening in the stock market. Without this connection, we're probably not much different than ants scurrying around in their little anthill. Without a spiritual life there is no meaning to life other than survival.

My Emotional Life: What Feels Good to Me?

What gives you pleasure? What makes you feel whole and complete? What's fun? What feeds your sense of self? What makes your heart open? What makes you feel creative instead of afraid? Flexible instead of rigid? Compassionate instead of judgmental? For most of us, we're our most emotionally healthy selves when we feel strong and loving and whole. You can have all the money in the world, but if your heart isn't open you'll have no one to love or be loved by. You can have all the money in the world, but if you're afraid of losing it and you don't trust yourself and others to protect it, it's not worth it. If you don't know what it's like to feel confident and resilient, you'll be afraid of every change that happens in your life.

My Physical Self: What Takes Care of Me?

Do you value your body—both mentally and physically—and therefore give yourself the physical care and stimulation your body and mind need? Your body and mind are a vehicle for carrying you through this life. You might take better care of your car—your vehicle with tires—than you take care of your physical body. You might take better care of your children's bodies than your own. You might take better care of your house than you take care of your body. You might be wonderfully evolved emotionally, but your body isn't going to make the long haul to old age. It really is quite simple. If you don't take care of your body, how will you travel in this life? What's the point of a lot of money if you don't have a "vehicle" to travel in? One eighty-four-year-old man I know bemoaned, "If I had known I was going to live this long, I would have taken better care of my teeth." You don't get a another set of teeth. If you don't nourish your brain cells, they'll die. How are you going to think and make decisions? You don't get another physical body. If you want to "travel" in this vehicle—your body—to age eighty-five and beyond, you need to take care of yourself.

My Financial Life: How Will I Pay for My Life?

Money is the tool that pays for the roof over your head, the food for your body, and the doctor when you're ill. Without adequate money, it's difficult to take care of your body and it's difficult to live creatively. Without adequate money it's difficult to live a purposeful life that's value-based. Money is the means to provide for your basic physical needs. Money allows you to protect yourself—to give yourself food, clothing, and shelter. Money also provides for your emotional needs. It allows you to pay for things of beauty and pleasure. Money is an integral facet of life-planning for retirement.

Balance Is Essential

The need to balance the spiritual, emotional, physical, and financial facets in your life-planning for retirement is essential. If these four facets are not in balance, life-planning cannot work.

There are two emotions that have the capacity to destroy your life balance in any of these four facets.

Fear is the first emotion. When my friend Adam said, "I've never been worse," he was describing his own fear. Hopelessness and despair are other manifestations of fear. Adam was feeling fear because of the drop in his portfolio. Sometimes fear also shows itself as anxiety.

Several years ago I was at a dinner, sitting next to a well-known psychiatrist. We began chatting about our work and mutual acquaintances. Then he said to me, "Keep doing what you're doing, Ruth. Do you know that panic attacks are absolutely epidemic right now? And no one is really talking about them. It's as if it were a secret illness. And we're not acknowledging how many people's lives are truly handicapped by this condition. Based on my experience," the doctor continued, "I believe that about 90 percent of panic attacks are caused by money and money concerns."

A panic attack is the body responding to some kind of fear. A panic attack, according to doctors, can be sucking your breath in sharply as you hear a new noise in your car, when the warranty just ran out, and asking yourself, "Now, how will I ever pay for this?" A panic attack can be waking up at two o'clock in the morning in a cold sweat, with trouble breathing, wondering if your job will be safe during the company downsizing. Or wondering if your child, who has been breaking curfew lately and still isn't home tonight, could really be in trouble. Or wondering how long you'll be able to keep working at your job, since you really don't have much money put away for retirement. Or wondering how low the stock market really will go. Or wondering if that low-grade fever you've had for a few days could really be something serious.

Some people express fear as denial: "Whatever I do, it doesn't work, so why try? I've tried to earn more money. Doesn't work. I've tried to keep money in savings. Someone always needs the money. There's nothing to do. I just won't think about it." That's money denial, which comes out of fear.

Some people express fear as obsession: "It's not working. I don't have enough money for retirement, so I'll have to earn more. I know my children won't see me and I won't have time to get to the gym to work out, but that's the way it is. What I've been doing isn't working, so it's crunch time—for the next decade or two." Obsession was the expression of my friend Adam's fear. His plan was to focus all his energy on fixing his portfolio—even if it meant losing the balance in the rest of his life. Nothing seems to preoccupy the mind like worry over money—if you let it. Adam was letting fear take charge of his life.

Fear Isn't Rational

"I can't figure out what happened to all those years. I looked in the mirror this morning and I saw my father. I can't believe it!" This was Pat talking to me one morning in my office. "I can't imagine anything that I could do now would do any good anyway. I don't think I have enough years left."

That's fear.

"The last child is in college," Andrea told me. "I never thought we'd actually get here. All those years of running around with kids' activities. And we're here. Freedom! But when I looked at my husband this morning at breakfast, I saw a stranger. Truly a stranger. I have no idea what to talk to him about. It really frightens me. How can we live in the same house and not have anything to say? Maybe we won't make it."

That's fear.

"Ruth, you don't understand!" Laurel was very emphatic as she explained to me, "You keep wanting me to stop spending so much money and start saving. You keep asking me to raise my rates in my business. You keep telling me about SEP-IRAs and Roth IRAs, and I know you think they're important—but not now. I am the happiest, Ruth, when I don't have to think about money. Thinking about money makes me feel disconnected from the goodness of the Universe. I trust the Universe to provide whatever I need. So not now, Ruth. Right now I'm just not going to think about retirement."

That's denial. Remember, denial is a form of fear.

Greed is the second emotion that destroys the balance in life-planning. Greed is not a word that most people associate with themselves. And yet I've found that it is every bit as prevalent as fear, and every bit as destructive. It just isn't openly acknowledged.

Greed is expressed as, "Everyone else is taking a vacation. I should be able to as well. I don't care if I don't have the money, I'm going to do it anyway."

Greed is expressed as, "There must be an easier way—a shorter or faster way—to make money. I just have to be willing to take the risk."

Greed is expressed as, "The stock market is going up. The sky's the limit. I can sector invest and go for the highest return."

Greed is expressed as, "If I want it, I should be able to get it."

In the late 1990s, we saw greed in the highest levels of some U.S. corporations. Greed took over to the degree that there seemed to be no connection between the person at the top and the workers or shareholders. We all understood this as pure and simple greed. The two questions asked by the media—and by regular folks like you and me— were "Don't they have any principles?" and "How much money does one person need?"

Greed Isn't Rational

Also, in the 90s, individuals—you and I—got greedy. We, as an investing society, acted as if there were no core principles of money. (We'll talk more about these principles in chapter 9.) We acted as if this time period was different, and the core principles of money were passé. Articles were written about the possibility that maybe sector investing—rather than diversification—was the way to go. And many, many responded with greed. They threw out their diversification plans and followed the money. Greed, like fear, isn't rational.

Greed, like fear, causes people to take actions that are not based on principles. Greed, like fear, destroys any kind of life-planning strategy because people throw out their plans and follow the greed.

"I know my investment portfolio is down by half. I know I should have followed my plan. I know I shouldn't have moved so much money into those kinds of companies," Robert explained with great insistence. "But, Ruth, you should've heard the returns the guys at the club said they were getting. I felt like I was being stupid. I didn't want to get left behind."

That's greed.

"We just want what everyone else has, Ruth." Barry and his wife, Jan, were in my office together. "All our friends are taking trips all over," Barry explained. "So we just booked tickets to Italy for the whole family. We're going in a few weeks. I know we don't have the money. I know we don't need any more debt on our credit cards. I know I need to increase my 401(k) contribution, but, Ruth, really! Everyone else gets to do these things, we should be able to as well."

"I agree with Barry," Jan interjected. "No one else seems to worry about those things, so we aren't either. Our kids deserve nice things and so do we. Whatever it takes."

That's greed.

"Ruth, the old rules just don't apply anymore," David said, trying to explain why he changed his long-term investment strategy. "I think we're in a different time with different rules. I don't think it's possible to make money the old-fashioned way. I don't want to feel stupid by doing that when it won't work. I changed what I was doing because I just couldn't bear losing so much money. I think I can figure out when to get in and out of the stock market. And besides, I think I can make money faster than the old way."

That's fear and greed together. Do you see it?

Greed and fear will destroy any life-plan that you create. Fear and greed insidiously and completely skew any kind of balance you have in your spiritual, emotional, physical, and financial life.

Think about it! In a growth or bull market in this country, greed is the norm. People destroy their balanced, diversified financial plans and chase whatever is making the most money. They think, "I'm afraid I'll be left behind," so they follow their greed.

In a recessionary or bear market in this country, fear is the norm. Once again, people destroy their balanced, diversified financial plans and hide from the market, rather like a child hiding from the boogeyman. They think, "This is way too scary. I may lose all of my money. I'm just going to take my money and run." They cash in their stock portfolios and put their money into a bond or money market account so they feel safe.

Then, of course, as it always does, the market reverses. The stock market starts to grow. Welcome back, greed!

Greed and fear are the primary reasons people don't make money. Both of these emotions really say the same thing: "This could go on forever." When the stock market is going up, greed says, "Get on board! The market will keep going up!" When the stock market is going down, fear says, "Get off! It's going to crash!"

In September of 2001, after the market had taken a precipitous dive, my twenty-six-year-old son told me that he was thinking about moving his 401(k) money out of balanced growth mutual funds and into a guaranteed certificate within his 401(k) plan. When I asked him why, he said, "Because my money just keeps going down."

"But, honey," I said, "that's what always happens in a bear market. In a bear market, the market goes down. It contracts. It reconfigures. It's normal and it's healthy in a capitalistic system. The market can't always be growing, just like a person can't always be extroverted. One needs to have some introverted time. Economically, a bear market is the introverted time and the extroverted time is a growth market or a bull market."

The *emotional* key to a bear market is to not make decisions out of fear. People always have regrets when they make decisions out of fear. The *financial* key to a bear market is to keep to the principles of money and stay with a diversified plan.

The *emotional* key to a growth or bull market is to not make decisions out of greed. People always have regrets when they make decisions out of greed. The *financial* key to a bull market is the same as for a bear market—keep to the principles of money and stay with a diversified plan. (Again, we'll cover the principles of money in chapter 9.)

I also told my son that if he could find within himself some courage during this bear market, he should increase his contribution to his 401(k) plan because, since the market was down so far, the shares he was buying in his mutual funds were actually on sale. I told him he could think of it as a two-for-one sale in the stock market. I also told him that he had better get used to these alternating bear and bull cycles—and he had better find a way to not get into either fear or greed—because he was probably going to go through at least six more of these cycles before he would need the money for retirement.

What I told my son is true. There are normal cycles to all of life—in all facets—spiritual, emotional, physical, and financial. Some parts of the cycles feed fear and some feed greed. If you can learn to recognize both of these emotions—in your friends, in the media, and in yourself—and be vigilant to not live your life dictated by either of these emotions, your life-planning will succeed.

To be vigilant, you have to be able to recognize fear and greed in yourself—and to name them for what they are.

When did I last feel fear in such a way that I decided—or almost decided—to act based on that fear? What happened? What did I do?

When did I last feel greed in such a way that I decided—or almost decided—to act based on greed? What happened? What did I do?

> How will I make sure that I don't ever let either of these emotions skew my perspective of life and destroy my balanced life-plan?

Learning to manage greed and fear is an essential life-planning skill.

CHAPTER SIX

Creating a New Vision

But if you travel far enough,
one day, you will recognize yourself coming down the road
to meet yourself. And you will say . . . yes.
—Marion Woodman

Diane was sitting across the desk from me in my office. Recently divorced, she had just told me that at the age of forty-nine she was feeling really old.

"You're not old, Diane," I told her. "Fifty is midlife. You have half your life to go."

Diane gave a little laugh and said, "I truly don't know whether that should relieve me or scare me. Or maybe it should do a little bit of both."

Then I said to her, "Diane, you need to form a different picture in your mind of what the fifties will be like for you—and the sixties and the seventies and the eighties and maybe even the nineties. So, let me ask you a question: What do you want your life to be like, say, 30 years from now?"

"You really are trying to scare me, aren't you?" she said. We both laughed, and then she answered my question. "I don't know. I only know I don't want my life in my seventies to be like my mom's. My mother was divorced later in her life. That divorce was a financial disaster for her. She developed a medical condition for which she needed care. She didn't have long-term care insurance, and she didn't have any money or assets, so the government paid for her care. The care the government provided was nursing home care, so she went into a nursing home probably about four years before she really needed to be there. She was able to keep $48 per month from her Social Security check to pay for all her personal expenses. She was broke and felt trapped. Without help from her children, she wouldn't even have been able to buy clothes for herself, much less gifts for her grandkids. Even though she was grateful for the help, she knew she had lost her independence. She expressed her unhappiness frequently and, for a time, that unhappiness tested her spiritual beliefs."

She gave a big sigh as she said again, "I only know I don't want old age to be like my mom's. Her seventies were hard on her and sad for me."

"So," I asked again, "what do you want your life to be like—30 years from now?"

It was a good question. It's a good question for all my clients. It's a good question for you too.

Most people know what they *don't* like and *don't* want to do, but they don't have an idea of what they *do* like and *do* want to do. They have no picture—no vision—of what they want their life to be. They are so busy dealing with that day-to-dayness of life, they, like Diane, have no time to think about age seventy-nine.

"Intellectually, I know I have to think about how my life is going to work 30 years from now," Diane said, responding to my question. "I also know that waiting until I am seventy to think about age seventy-nine isn't going to work either. I know I need to form a picture for those years that is different from the picture I learned from my mother," Diane concluded.

Life-planning involves forming a picture of what you are trying to create. Without a picture, you may know what you *don't* want, just like Diane knew she didn't want her seventies to be like her mom's. But you, like Diane, may not have any idea of what that different picture might be.

You've already learned in this book that if you can control your emotions, you can control your life.

You've learned that if you're willing to practice the resiliency—to be able to estimate what will happen—and flexible, you can make life-planning work.

You've learned that life-planning is multifaceted—with spiritual, emotional, physical, and financial aspects. To make your life-planning work, all facets have to be in balance. And you've learned you must hold that balance in the face of two destructive emotions—fear and greed.

Now you're understanding how important it is to have a clear vision of what you want life to be during the third and final stage of your life. Like many people you may know what you *don't* want. But you may not know what you *do* want.

Most People Retire *From* Something But They Don't Know What They Are Retiring *To*

A picture of what you are trying to create is necessary for all three stages of life, but it's especially important for the last stage of life—the stage called retirement. Most of us spend a lot of time and effort in stage one preparing for life in stage two—educating ourselves, advancing in our jobs, developing relationships, or simply dreaming about love and kids and houses and travel. But in stage two, we don't do much to prepare for stage three—except for building our retirement savings plans. In stage two, we don't generally dream about the pleasures and achievements of stage three. If we do dream about stage three while in stage two of our lives, it's usually about getting away from something we don't like rather than dreaming about what we'd like to do and achieve. Quite simply, most people retire *from* something, but they don't know what they are retiring *to*. Among the three stages, stage three is unique in this respect.

Even before the actual birth of a child, there's anticipation. We think about all the possibilities in the first stage of that child's life. That anticipation continues as the child grows to young adulthood and increases as plans and dreams for stage two take shape. But then the anticipation that has been so much a part of life up until this point changes. This change happens because most adults in stages one and two of their lives see retirement—the third stage—in two phases. Most of them see the first phase—the beginning of retirement—as a time of freedom from everything they didn't like in stage two of their lives. This phase of retirement looks quite pleasant. They don't have to go to work, set an alarm clock, or be with people they don't like. No one tells them what to do, and they don't have to stay caught up with paperwork.

The more you disliked those aspects of your work life, the more you anticipate the absence of them. You might even be able to have fun—you say to yourself—do a little traveling, play some golf, work in the garden, take a class, see the grandkids. Freedom. The only real unpleasantness is the worry that this phase of retirement will be too short and that you won't have enough time to enjoy your freedom before the dreaded second phase begins.

How do I picture this first phase of retirement? What am I retiring *from*? Does that seem pleasant to me? How do I define freedom in this phase of my retirement?

From the perspective of stage two of our lives, people don't anticipate the second phase of retirement. The second phase of retirement means that at any time—and you don't know when or where—something bad could happen and your freedom could be over. This dreaded second phase of retirement might start with a medical crisis. You could break your hip. You may develop a chronic or fatal illness. You may have to move and go to "the home." Or this dreaded second phase of retirement may start when your partner dies and suddenly you're alone. Maybe you can't pay the bills. Maybe you can't afford to stay independent. Maybe you can't afford to travel anymore, or you may be too scared to travel because of your health. Maybe the money is disappearing too fast and you have to move. Now where will you live? And what kind of care will you need? What if you can't afford good care? Then what?

This unpleasant picture of the second phase of retirement is one many people hold.

Ask yourself:

What is my picture of this second phase of retirement?

What am I afraid might happen that could make this phase of my life unpleasant?

What do I worry about?

My client Barbara is an example. "I'm afraid," Barbara explained to me one day in my office, "that when I actually get to retire, I'll already be so old that I won't have time to do anything fun. I can just see getting some serious illness like cancer that will take all my money and whatever time I have left. Then it will all be over. That's what happened to my mom, and I'm afraid it will happen to me."

Another client, John, told me, "My dad said he wanted to work part-time until he was seventy and golf part-time. Then at seventy or so, he wanted to golf full-time because he wanted to die on the golf course. He figured that was the same as dying in heaven. Well, it didn't work that way. He was laid off the year before he could've retired to part-time, and because he didn't have work income—even part-time work income—he had to resign from the country club where he and his buddies had played golf for years. He went to a public course, but his buddies weren't there. At age seventy he was diagnosed with congestive heart failure. He died from complications of open-heart surgery. It was all very hard, and I'm afraid that will happen to me."

Beth told me this: "When my aunt and uncle were in their late sixties, my uncle had a stroke. He was hospitalized for a long time, and then there was rehab. When he returned home, my aunt needed help to care for him. He was a big man. Finally, my uncle had to go into a nursing home. My aunt had one of two choices. She could watch their money disappear for all the nursing home costs, or she could divorce my uncle and at least keep half of what was left for her remaining years. It was terrible. She couldn't divorce him. She just couldn't, even though she knew she should. She ended up on government assistance—and still is. She seems like she has a very hard life."

Kari expressed her fears this simply: "I'm afraid I'll run out of money and that I'll need help and no one will be there to help me. That's it!"

Again, ask yourself:

What am I afraid of?

To life-plan successfully, it's important to be clear about your worries and fears so you can create a picture that addresses them. This picture is called a vision statement, and it will show the life you want to create. This picture isn't about fear and unpleasantness. It's a statement of what kind of life you want— really want—to create for yourself.

A Vision Statement Is the Beginning of Change

A vision statement is a powerful tool for change, because it literally creates a picture in your brain that helps your brain to see something different from what your eyes have seen. A vision statement gives words—power tools for the brain—to what you want, so the brain can see a positive picture. A vision statement will help you see a new way of being in retirement. If you don't give your brain a new picture, your brain has only the old picture—the one you've seen by watching others in retirement. For me, that would be my grandmother. For Diane, that would be her mother.

Remember in chapter 1 when you thought about your vision of retirement learned from your role models? You also thought about what you liked about that picture of retirement and what you didn't like. Up until now, that learning—from your role models—is the only picture your brain has had. If that picture of

retirement isn't what you want for *your* life, now's your cr.
to envision something different.

When I asked my client, Diane, what she wanted her life to
be like 30 years from now, she looked stumped. I said, "I'll tell
you what my vision statement is for the last third of my life." I
told her, "I want to be feisty, strong-willed, loved, and lovable. I
want to matter to someone—to be needed by someone. I want
enough money so I will have choices about where I live and be
able to pay for care—if I need it. And I want to wear really big
hats."

As I was speaking, Diane's face broke out into a big grin.

"So now it's your turn, Diane," I told her. "Keep it simple
and make it sound like you—your personality."

"Okay," she responded. "I'll give it a try. Here goes: When I
am seventy-nine, and before, I want to live in a small condo so I
can be gone a lot and not worry about taking care of it. I want
to have a lot of money and be very healthy so I can travel all
over the world. There are so many places I want to see." She
stopped to give me an explanation, "I feel so stuck right now in
my job and keeping up my house. I want to feel more freedom
30 years from now. More freedom than I've ever had. There,"
she said quite forcibly, "that's my vision. That's it!"

"Good start, Diane." I told her. "Good start."

It takes courage to create a different picture—to create
change. Even if you have no idea how you'd actually make it
happen, see if you can find the courage to create a new vision—
a new picture for your life. Remember, to have a truly great
retirement, you must believe in yourself and your ability to
manage your emotional response to events in your life. You must
believe in your ability to be resilient and in your ability to
manage fear and greed. And, you must believe in your ideas
and be willing to form a new picture—a vision for the third stage
of your life.

Epictetus, a Stoic philosopher, talked about the vision
statement as a first step when he said, "First say to yourself what
you would be; and then do what you have to do."

To be what you want to be, you need a vision. It's time to create your personal vision statement.

First, picture yourself in the last stage of your life—stage 3. Then answer the question that I asked my client, Diane: "So, what do you want your life to be like—10, 20, 30 and maybe even 40 years from now?"

Make this statement very specific. Remember, you are literally creating a picture of what you want to create in the future. Ask yourself:

If I could create whatever I wanted for this last third of my life, what would that life look like, feel like, and be like—in all four facets of my life—emotionally, physically, spiritually, and financially?

Write down your answer to that question.

What you just wrote is your first attempt at creating your own personal vision statement. This vision statement will help give direction, purpose, and meaning to your life-planning for stage three. If it doesn't, go back and rethink the question. A clear vision statement is important, because you'll use it again in chapters 11, 12, 13, and 14, when you put together all the information and skills you've learned in these chapters and actually develop specific, decade-by-decade strategies for your retirement life.

CHAPTER TWO

Who Am I?

Somewhere along the line of development we discover what we really are, and then we make our real decision for which we are responsible. Make that decision primarily for yourself because you can never really live anyone else's life. . . . The influence you exert is through your own life and what you become yourself.
—*Eleanor Roosevelt*

There's no shortcut to successful life-planning. We might wish we could find some magic formula and put ourselves and our money into that formula and—*viola!*—our life works! Clients of mine say: "Just tell me *how much* money I need so I can retire, Ruth." Or, "Just tell me *where* to put my money so I will have enough for retirement, and I'll do it."

Life isn't that simple. There are no simple answers to managing your money, and there are no simple answers to life-planning. A simple, generic formula for a successful life just isn't possible. Remember our discussion of fear and greed in chapter 5? Fear and greed destroy your life balance. Fear and greed also make us want to believe there's some magic formula for making our lives work.

Greed tells us, "There must be a faster way, an easier way." Greed makes an intelligent person believe that a simple formula can work for every John and Jane—and that it can work for you, too. Greed makes you vulnerable to trusting opportunists who will take your money and promise you more than they can deliver. Greed makes you forget that if "it sounds too good to be true," it probably is. Greed stops you from doing your work. Greed makes you think simplistically. Greed is dangerous to the successful life-planning process.

Fear tells us, "This is too hard. I'll never earn enough money. I'll never be able to figure out how to invest my money in the right place." Fear destroys your focus. Fear creates excuses. Fear destroys your creativity and hope. Fear stops you, as an intelligent person, from taking the actions necessary for making your life work. Fear is dangerous to your successful life-planning process.

If you need help managing your fear or greed, go back and reread chapter 5.

If you want to develop a life-plan that really works, you have to put fear and greed aside and start to plan. In order to successfully life-plan you need more information—much more information. This chapter is the first of three information-gathering chapters. In this chapter, you will gather information about *you*—who you are and what you like. Then, in chapter 8 you'll gather information about your *work*. And in chapter 9, you'll gather information about *money*.

This chapter will assist you in gathering information about yourself.

What is the most important information you need to successfully life-plan? No, it's not about which mutual fund in which to invest your 401(k) money. And it's not about how to pick a financial planner. It's not even about how to get your partner to learn to budget. It's about *you*! *You* are the only constant in stages one, two, and three of your life. *You* are the only consistent ingredient in all facets of life-planning—spiritual, emotional, physical, and financial. *You!* The more you know and understand about you, the better and more successful your decision-making will be for the third stage of your life.

By gathering information about yourself, you're starting on a process of self-discovery that will provide the data to help you successfully plan your life. Again, there's no shortcut to accumulating this information—there's never a shortcut to growth and discovery.

You Are the Only Constant in Your Life

Aristotle said, "Know thyself." This admonition is truly critical in developing a new retirement model. You need to understand who you are and what you need to be spiritually, emotionally, physically, and financially healthy. The more you know about yourself, the better decisions you will make. If you aren't clear about who you really are, you may end up making decisions that don't work at all. Remember Art, in chapter 1? When he made his retirement decision, he didn't understand himself enough to know that he wouldn't be happy without his golf and his lunches. By the time he realized this about himself, those golf and lunch relationships had already ended, and he didn't know how to replace them. He felt alone and unhappy and broke. The decision he made may have worked for someone else—with different needs. But the decision he made did not work for him.

You have to be willing to take the time to think clearly about you, so you can use that information when you strategize for stage three. You need to be clear about what you need. Think about what you like and don't like—about what gives you pleasure, about what's fun. The following self-assessment is about you. *Not* who you think you *should be*. *Not* who you think you *will be*. *Not* who you think *other* people think you are. This self-assessment is about who you really are *right now*. You may be so busy with your life that you haven't thought about these questions for a long time—if ever. It's time to think about them now.

As you are answering these questions about you, remember, you're an evolving creative person, so these answers may change over time. Don't worry about that. Just think about who you are today—this wonderful, complex person—*you*. Answer them with what you know about you—right now, where you are.

If you're in a committed relationship, each of you should answer these questions. First, though, answer the questions individually—it's too easy for you to tell your partner who he or she is and for your partner to tell you who you are. After you've answered the questions individually—then and only then—talk together about your answers.

Information Gathering About Myself

Some of the following questions may be difficult because you've never thought about them before. That's okay. Just take your time. If you get stuck on a question, move on and come back to that question later. These questions are asking you to think about yourself in a new way—with a new understanding.

What gives me pleasure? What's fun? What makes me happy?

What stimulates my thinking? What do I do that makes me think and feel smart?

Who stimulates my thinking? Who makes me think and feel smart?

What have I always wanted to learn?

What have I always wanted to do? What have I always wanted to experience?

When do I feel needed? What makes me feel valuable and important?

What makes me feel safe? When and where do I feel at peace?

What creates anxiety for me? When do I feel unsafe? What makes me feel worried?

Where is home to me? What makes that place home to me? Where do I want to live that feels beneficial to living long and healthy?

Who do I like to be with? Who is fun and pleasurable?

Who makes me feel healthy and good about myself?

Who do I *not* want to be with? Who drains me?

What do I want to be remembered for when I die? What will I want to have done that will be remembered? What difference will I have made?

Now, looking back over your answers to these questions, think about what you learned about yourself.

What questions were more difficult to answer?

Why were they difficult?

What is the most important *new* information that I learned from asking these questions?

What is absolutely important for me *not* to forget about myself as I begin to plan my life?

If Art had asked himself these questions, he would have made different life-planning decisions and the outcome could have been different.

Knowing yourself and what's important to you is necessary information for successful life-planning.

What Is Work?

Everyone's work, whether it be literature or music or pictures or architecture or anything else, is always a portrait of the self.
—Samuel Butler

Less than half of baby boomers are happy with their current jobs. If this is true for you, it's no wonder you want to believe in the finish-line model of retirement. That model allows you to know when you can leave your "miserable" and "life-restricting" work life.

Many years ago, I was a young teacher in a large public school system. When I had taught for about three and a half years, I decided it was time for me to retire from public school teaching and move on to something else. I was twenty-six.

At my farewell party, a social studies teacher from my school, who was in his early sixties, asked me, "Why, in heaven's name, are you quitting teaching?"

I told him the truth. I said that I enjoyed the teaching but didn't find teaching within a large school system effective and rewarding. "The plain truth is," I said, "I don't like it."

"But," he said, "I heard you're a really good teacher!"

"Thanks," I said, "but I really don't like it. It's time for me to do something that will be more fulfilling."

"But you can't leave," he protested. "I didn't. And I've never liked teaching. Actually," he continued, "I've always disliked this job."

I wasn't surprised. I had heard this man was a poor teacher who didn't seem to care much about his students.

"You should've left years ago, like I am doing now," I told this teacher.

"That's preposterous," he fumed. "I stayed because of the government retirement. Best retirement in the country. Would never give that up. It took me thirty-two years, but I made it. I retire in less than two years."

That teacher's life-planning for retirement was the finish-line model. That's the model where you are willing to stay in a job you don't like for as many years as it takes to get to the finish line and then retire.

If you're following the finish-line model and you're staying until retirement in a job you don't like, you're paying two prices.

The first price is that you're miserable, just like this teacher had been for 32 years. And your partner probably never stops hearing about it—so your partner is miserable too. And your kids never stop hearing about it, and neither do your friends. Are you miserable? Whining? Crabby? Unhappy? Resentful? Pick your emotion. If you're doing work that is not fulfilling, everyone knows the price you're paying to make the money to provide a living and get a retirement. That's misery—for everyone.

The other day in my office I was talking to a young couple, Armando and Betsy—both of them right in the middle of stage two. Yes, forty is young! They had made an appointment because Armando had just been laid off from his job. They were trying to determine what to do without his six-figure salary.

"You know," Betsy spoke first, "as frightening as it is to have Armando laid off, it is also somewhat of a relief."

"What are you talking about?" Armando interrupted.

"Because," Becky continued, avoiding Armando's eyes by looking at me, "he has been miserable to live with. When he comes home from work—which is always late—he spends at least an hour complaining about how hard his job is and how impossible the people at work are. After he eats, he goes to bed early because he's so exhausted, leaving me to wash the dishes and get the kids to bed. On weekends he sleeps late both days and is very grumpy. He never does anything around the house. He gets mad if I ask him to do something. It's been very hard and, to tell you the truth, it's been lonely and depressing.

"Since he's been laid off," Becky continued, "we've been to two movies. We took the kids to the Science Museum. We've gone out to dinner a couple of times. It's like when we first met, except for the kids, of course. I know I should be worried about the money and I know he has to get another job, but this is so much better."

I looked at Armando. "Any truth to what she's saying?"

"Well, maybe a slight exaggeration," Armando replied. "But, I guess it's pretty close to the truth. I *have* been pretty miserable. I had planned to stay in this job until I retired. I wish this were retirement, that it wasn't a temporary layoff. For the first time in my life, I wish I were old. I can't stand the thought of getting another job like my old job."

"Me neither," said Becky.

Just like Becky and Armando, the first price you pay when you stay in a job you don't like is unhappiness.

Studies show that people who were miserable during much of their lives don't have the greatest chances at longevity. This is the second price you may pay for the finish-line model of retirement. Staying until retirement in a job that makes you miserable means that you, like that poor social studies teacher, will probably have only four or five good years as a reward for being miserable for most of your adult work life.

So, again, the price you pay for living with the finish-line model is that you're less happy than you'd be if you had fulfilling work. And when you finally get to the finish line—which is the goal—you probably won't live long after that. The payoff for years of unhappiness is way too little for most people. It's just not worth it. The finish-line model doesn't factor in all the facets of healthy living—spiritual, emotional, physical, and financial. In the finish-line model of retirement, those facets are not in balance. That's why that model doesn't work. That's why it's time for a new model.

Work Is a Productive Activity

How you define *work* is critical to this new life-planning model. You will need a broad, holistic definition of work. The broad definition of work we'll use for life-planning purposes is: **Work is a productive activity that makes me feel like I'm doing something useful**.

This definition means that when you work, something gets done, and getting it done makes you feel like what you have done has some value, to someone, somehow. It means you feel some kind of satisfaction when you are working or have finished work.

By the way, this definition of work does not just apply to stage three. This is a definition of work that can be used for any stage of your life—including stage three.

There are many different kinds of work—some work you do *without* pay and some you do *for* pay. For some, mowing the lawn is work—could be paid or unpaid. Other forms of work could be changing a diaper, lifting weights, delivering meals-on-wheels, writing a book, fixing a pothole in the road, reading to children, cutting someone's hair, cooking a meal, calculating someone's taxes, singing in the choir, managing a company or a department in a company, teaching kids, counseling someone, driving a car—you get the idea.

You have to know how *you* define work. What does it mean to have productive work—to you? What does it mean to feel useful or to feel satisfied—to you? Since you'll need and you'll want to have some form of work for your entire life, you have to understand what work means to you. It doesn't matter what work means to anyone else. You have to understand what work means to *you*.

It's time for more information gathering. In chapter 7, you did a self-assessment—gathering information about you as a person. Now in chapter 8, you will do a work assessment—gathering information about the activities you do or can do that are productive and feel useful to you. This assessment is to help you understand your definition of work—paid work and unpaid work.

Take time to think about these questions. Your answers are important data about you and your work that you'll need for successful life-planning.

Information Gathering About My Work

Ask yourself the following questions. Again, as in the last chapter, some of these questions may be difficult because you've never thought about them before. Don't get stuck. It's important that you understand your work and your relationship to that work.

What is my work-for-pay? What do I do for income?

What does my work-for-pay give me? How does my work-for-pay feed me?

Answer these questions using all four facets of a healthy life.

1. How does my work feed me spiritually?

2. How does my work feed me emotionally?

3. How does my work feed me physically?

4. How does my work feed me financially?

What does my work-for-pay *take from* me? How does my work-for-pay restrict my life? How does this work drain me? How does my work-for-pay make me un-happy?

1. Spiritually?

2. Emotionally?

3. Physically?

4. Financially?

What is my work that is *not*-for-pay? (This can be work at home or it can be volunteer work that's not at home. Be sure to include all your work that is without pay.)

What does my not-for-pay work *give* me? How does my work that's not-for-pay feed me?

1. Spiritually?

2. Emotionally?

3. Physically?

4. Financially?

What does my work that is not-for-pay *take from* me? How does my not-for-pay work restrict my life? How does this work drain me? How does my work that is not for-pay make me unhappy?

1. Spiritually?

2. Emotionally?

3. Physically?

4. Financially?

What are my strengths? What am I really good at?

A strength could be the ability to learn new information. Your list of strengths could also include that you're creative, that you're a good problem solver, that you're dedicated and dependable. A strength could be that you have a good appearance, that you have the ability to organize, that you have the ability to be flexible. A strength could be that you get along well with people.

So, again, what are my strengths?

What are my weaknesses? What am I not as good at?

A weakness could be not being able to take criticism. A weakness could be that your health is poor, so consistency is difficult. It could be that you have difficulty being flexible—you're too rigid. You might have trouble learning new procedures or new ways to do things. You might be moody—you have trouble managing your emotions.

So, again, what are my weaknesses?

You've learned a lot about yourself with these questions, right? Now ask yourself:

What kind of work is good for me? (This is work that makes me feel good.)

What kind of work drains me? (This is work that makes me unhappy.)

How could I make enough money *and* be able to do more of the work that *feels good* to me? (Brainstorm ideas.)

How could I make enough money *and* do less of the work that *drains* me? (Brainstorm ideas.)

As you do your life-planning, it's essential that you understand your concept of work because, using this definition of work (work is a productive activity that makes me feel like I'm doing something useful), you will always have some kind of work in your life—paid or unpaid. And in a healthy life-plan you need *some* work that you *truly* love. The work that you love may not always be your work-for-pay. But the work that you love has to be in your life—somewhere. The work you love may be hanging wallpaper, it may be figuring out tax forms, it may be weeding the garden, or it may be teaching second graders. But it has to be somewhere.

It's also essential that you understand that no work you do should make you miserable. If your work makes you miserable, you need to make an appointment with a vocational or career counselor and figure out what work you *can* do in your life that will give you some degree of satisfaction and purpose. You need to do this now! With a healthy life-planning model you won't have to wait until retirement to get out of your miserable job. That's the finish-line model. It doesn't work! You've already learned that. If you're miserable in your work, get some help to find a new kind of work. Now! Don't wait. Get some help.

You have now gathered data about your *work* (this chapter) and about *you* (chapter 7). In the next chapter (chapter 9) you will focus on your *money*. Later in this book, you will use these three different sets of data to help you create a life-plan that will be successful.

CHAPTER NINE

Will It Ever Be Enough?

We live in the richest country in world history,
yet only about 5 percent of the population
ever achieves financial independence.
The problem is not the high cost of living.
It's the cost of living high.
—Michael LeBoeuf

I truly believe that the vast majority of us will *not* be able to save enough money in the first two stages of our lives to prepay for the entire last stage of our lives. In other words, the majority of us will *not* be financially independent at or before the age of sixty-five. That means the majority of us will not have enough money to completely retire from our work-*for-pay* lives at age sixty-five. We simply won't have enough money to have a good life without any financial worries for 25 to 35 years. Most people—maybe even you—don't want to hear this. And yet most of us know, if we told ourselves the truth, this information is true.

As long as we've started with bad news, let's continue with the bad news about money. What else *don't* we want to know?

Careers Are Less Secure

The work environment of most people today is less stable than it was for the generations before us. This is true for two primary reasons. First, people change careers more often—a minimum of six times and quite possibly a dozen times. Studies tell us that if you're in the late part of stage one or the early part of stage two, about three-fourths of the career changes you will make haven't even been thought of yet. Fascinating!

The second reason the work environment of today is less secure is that companies themselves are in greater flux. More companies are acquiring other companies. Companies restructure more frequently. Because of this, there's less company loyalty to the employee than there used to be.

Defined-Contribution Plans
Are *NOT* Being Adequately Funded

Fewer defined-benefit retirement plans—plans where the retired worker gets a set amount of money every month—are available for employees. Because of this, most workers find themselves responsible for their own retirements by investing through defined-contribution retirement plans. The most common defined-contribution plans are 401(k) plans—for employees of for-profit companies—and 403(b) plans—for employees of not-for-profit companies. SEP-IRA and SIMPLE plans are for self-employed workers. Regular IRAs, Roth IRAs and deferred compensation plans are other ways to invest for retirement. Even though these defined-contribution retirement plans are effective vehicles for putting away money for retirement, studies show that fewer workers participate in defined-contribution retirement plans than in defined-benefit retirement plans. Only 23 percent of eligible employees contribute to their 401(k) plans. Of the 36 percent of the labor force that is eligible for a defined-benefit retirement plan, roughly 80 percent participate in the plans. Why the significant difference? When a retirement plan is flexible or optional, employees delay putting money into these plans until they think they have extra money after they pay their bills. This means, bottom line, that when a plan is optional, they put away less money for the future than they should. They put money away for fewer years than they should. And, they stop putting money into retirement plans when they need the money for regular expenses—so money accumulates less consistently.

Home Equity Is *NOT* Retirement Money

Many people consider the equity in their home—this is the value of the home they own—to be part of their retirement money.

If this has been a part of your thinking you might feel more secure because you think you have more money than you really do. But, very practically, including home equity as part of retirement planning does *not* work. Don't forget that you'll need a roof over your head for as long as you're alive. Even downsizing is more expensive than most think. You know this if you've ever priced the "single level, two bedroom, two bath with den" in that new townhome development for people over fifty-five years old. Home equity will most likely simply transfer to a paid-in-full, downsized home for your retirement. Home equity *may* provide a roof over your head in retirement, but it usually *cannot* provide money to pay your bills and expenses.

Inflation Is a Factor in Retirement Planning

Inflation is alive and well and needs to be factored into your retirement planning. Very simply, let me tell you how to do that. Let's say that you are fifty years old today. And let's assume that you need $25,000 a year now to pay your bills and expenses. That's not a lot of money by today's standards. However, let's see what inflation does to that $25,000. Figuring a modest 3 percent overall inflation rate, in 25 years—when you are seventy-five years old—you will need $52,344 a year just to duplicate the same lifestyle that you have now with $25,000. That's inflation.

For previous generations of retirees, inflation wasn't a significant concern because individuals didn't live very long. Three percent inflation for just four or five years wasn't very significant. But in the longevity model, even low amounts of inflation can have a devastating effect over 20 to 30 years. The longer the period of time—the greater the effect of inflation. This is where longevity is the bad news.

Inflation is an even more significant factor for individuals in stage three of their lives because health care costs are increasing at a higher inflation rate than the rest of the economy. And individuals in stage three of their lives use health care at a higher rate than individuals in stages one and two. Prescription drug costs, for example, rose by 35 percent from 2000 to 2002. And these drug costs are expected to continue to climb at double-digit rates.

Social Security Benefits Are Vulnerable

You have probably read about concerns over how large the trust fund is for Social Security. Many articles have been written about the possible demise of the Social Security program. Some articles claim Social Security will be bankrupt by 2018, some say by 2030. Some say there isn't a problem at all. Others say that Social Security will always be there, but the benefits will be significantly reduced for everyone except the most destitute. In other words, if you don't need it, you won't get it.

Amid all the speculation, what I know for sure is that the viability of Social Security is totally dependent on the ability and the willingness of workers to support people in the last third of their lives—the retirees. That will be a challenge primarily because there won't be as many workers in the future paying into Social Security. By 2015, more money will go to retirees than the system will take in from workers. In 1945, there were 42 workers for every retiree. In contrast, it's projected that in 2020 there will be 2.4 workers for every retiree. So with fewer workers, the workers who are contributing had better be making *very* good incomes. That means that young people, the majority of whom are in public schools today, need to get a really good education *now* or they won't be qualified for good-paying jobs. If they are not paid well, their contributions to the Social Security system will be too low to support all the retirees. Then there *will* be a problem. A serious problem.

So, that's the bad news, or at least part of it.

It's time for a little good news.

You're Going to Live!

The good news is that you're going to live! You are going to live much longer than you ever thought you would. So before you start getting too depressed about all the bad news, remember—most of the bad news is the result of the good news. The good news is longevity. And because you'll be around a long time, there's still plenty of time to develop strategies to change the bad news. As you work with strategies for changing the bad money news, know that I believe personal finance is *at least* 80 percent self-management and less than 20 percent intellectual knowledge. In other words, we—with our behaviors—determine what to do or not to do with our money. So, if you find yourself resisting some of the strategies in this chapter, review the earlier chapters about the skills that are needed for life-planning and be willing to practice those skills.

The strategies for change in this chapter will work for you in any stage of life. These strategies work because they involve the key principles of money. They work whether our country is in a bull market or bear market. They work whether you're twenty-two or eighty-two. They work whether you're male or female. They'll help you to create a financially successful life-plan for retirement—and the years before.

Principle of Money #1: Spend Less Than You Earn

Spend less than you earn. Most people don't follow this first principle. Most people spend *all* that they earn—and *more* with the use of credit cards and lines of credit.

This principle is crucial because if you don't follow this principle, none of the other principles will work.

As a consumer, there's a lot of pressure on you to spend—as

much as you can and as often as you can. Consumers, right now, drive about two-thirds of this economy. The U.S. culture has taught that you should be able to have what you see in the ads— and that you should be able to have it *now.* This attitude leads to entitlement spending. The entitlement spending message is: "If you want it, you should be able to get it. Now!" You believe that you don't have to wait until you have the money. Credit cards and lines of credit allow you to get what you want when you want it. Your spending doesn't have to correspond to how much money you actually have.

And when you do spend, you feel patriotic. You listen to the news at night and see whether "consumer confidence" is up or down. Consumer confidence is simply a measure of how much consumers have spent in a given month. If consumer confidence is down, oh, no! Bad news for our country and its future! If consumer confidence is up, you're supporting your country and spending money, and everyone is happy. Everyone, that is, except you, when you open your next credit card statement and try to figure out how you're going to pay the bill.

It feels good to most people to get what they want and feel entitled to. However, if you intend to make your financial life-planning work, you have to be willing to change your spending patterns. You have to!

In 1989, when the United States was in a recessionary time, I got a call from a reporter at a local television station. He asked me what advice I was giving to my clients to get through the recession. I told him I was telling them to cut their spending, stash cash, and pay off their debts.

"Don't you think that's unpatriotic?" he asked. "If people don't spend, we'll never get out of this recession!"

"So," I replied, "I should tell my clients, 'Go hurt yourselves. Go spend all the money you can in the name of patriotism. This is your sacrifice—to shop—for the good of our country. Even if it stops you from being able to have a financially secure life'?"

"Well," he puzzled, "when you put it that way . . ."

I interrupted him. "The advice I give my clients doesn't

change whether we're in a recessionary market or a growth market. This is advice that works because it's based on the principles of money. The principles of money don't change with the economic markets. And long term, I truly believe that following these principles is also good for our country because it creates financially healthy, financially independent people. It's what we all want for our children and ourselves. Why would my advice be different from that?"

That was advice I gave in the recessionary market of 1989, and it's the advice I continue to give today.

All Change Starts with a Decision to Change

If you want to create a successful life-plan, you must be willing to follow the first principle of money: Spend less than you earn. By following this principle, you have made a decision to get your financial life in alignment with the principles of money. You make this decision because you want your earnings to support you now and when you're eighty. Of course, that means I have to mention the "B" word. You know what I mean: *budget.* If you prefer to call a budget a *money plan* or *cash-flow plan,* that's fine. What you call it isn't important. What you *do* is important. Figure out how much money you and your family spend every month. You need to know this so you can follow the first principle of money and spend less than you earn.

All change starts with a decision to change. If you haven't decided to change, no budget structure will work for you. You have to decide what you are willing to do and not willing to do to manage your money. It's up to you.

If you have decided to follow Principle of Money #1, you need to figure out how much you spend each month—your monthly budget—for the exercises you will do in chapters 11, 12, and 13.

This isn't a budgeting book, so you won't find many budgeting details here. However, you can find budget information in most financial books to help you figure out your own monthly budget.

The basic structure of a budget (with some examples) is this:

1. **Monthly fixed expenses:** mortgage, utilities, car payment.

2. **Weekly flexible expenses:** groceries, eating out, babysitting, household supplies.

3. **Non-monthly expenses that *have to* be paid sometime during the year:** insurances, taxes, car and home maintenance.

4. **Non-monthly expenses that you *want to* be able to do sometime during the year:** vacations, furniture, landscaping, clothes.

5. **Emergency savings:** money to fund a catastrophe such as a layoff or disability.

Those are the categories. Now make lists and add up the numbers. What is your total spending in all these categories?

With that amount of spending, are you able to put away for the future at least 10 percent of your gross income (that's your earned income *before* taxes are taken out) and still have enough net income (your income *after* taxes are taken out) to pay for the expenses of your life? That's the question. You have to be willing to work and rework the numbers in your budget until you can pay for all your expenses *after* you have put away for the future—stage three—*at least* 10 percent of your income.

Putting 10 percent away means that if you earn $2500 each month before taxes, you should put away *at least* $250 per month—every month. If you earn $6000 each month before taxes, you should put away *at least* $600 per month—every month.

If you can't put away at least 10 percent of the money you earn and still have enough to pay your bills, you need to lower your spending. What are you willing to spend less on? If you can't figure out how to spend less, then you need to ask yourself, how can I earn more income? One way or the other, you need to be able to pay for your life style and still put away at least 10 percent of your income for retirement.

Work the numbers. As you work the numbers, remember, you are continuing to affirm the decision to spend less than you earn—either by lowering your spending or raising your income. You are doing this so your life-planning can be a success.

Principle of Money #2: Invest the Difference

Remember, if you don't follow the first principle of money— spend less than you earn—you won't be able to follow the other principles of money.

To have an adequate amount of money for the last third of your life, you need to invest a *minimum* of 10 percent of your earned income—your gross income—if you're in stage one of your life. If you're in stage two and you don't have much money put away for stage three, you need to increase that amount to 15 percent. So, if you're forty-five years old, you need to invest at least 15 percent of your gross income. That's your challenge! The money you earn has to be enough to pay for your life today *and* to pay for your life in stage three. If there isn't enough money to do that right now, you need to cut back further on your spending or you need to find a way to increase your income. Decide to make the numbers work. Remember, you can't spend all your money for today's expenses, because you're planning to live a long time and will need some of that money for stage three.

The second principle of money is about investing money for the future. Long-term money has to be invested. Investing is different from saving.

Saving means the money is liquid—available—in a savings account or money market account. A savings account is where your emergency money is kept. You save so the money's there when you need it. This saved money is not expected to grow in substantial enough numbers to even keep up with inflation. If it does, wonderful. But that isn't the purpose of saved money. The word *savings* has the same root word as *safe*. Saved money— liquid money—is for you to feel safe. Saved money is not invested money for the future.

Invested money, on the other hand, is money you put away and expect to grow over the long term. This money is for a future agenda such as retirement—stage three. The following are two rules about invested money that you need to follow to be a successful investor.

Diversification Is Crucial

First, you need to follow a diversified plan with your invested money. A diversified plan means your money is spread into all categories of investments. With a diversified plan, you don't try to time the market. Timing the market means you try to decide when and where you can make money—right now—and as a result you keep moving money in and out of investments. Trying to time the market takes a lot of time, it costs significant fees, and it only gets you ahead a very small percent of the time anyway. Trying to time the market is a little like gambling with your money. If you want to gamble, go to Las Vegas.

Try diversification instead. Spread your money around into all categories of investments. When you diversify your money in this way, you are basically saying, "I know that at any time in this market there's a place to make my money grow. I'm not going to try to guess where it is—that's market timing. So I will need to have my money in as many investment categories as possible."

A diversified plan works whether the United States is in a growth period or in a recessionary period. In a diversified plan you'll divide your investment money into three broad categories—stocks, bonds, and cash. When you invest in stocks, you are buying *ownership* in businesses. When you invest in bonds, you are *loaning* money to businesses or to some form of our government. We'll talk more about cash later in this chapter.

A long-term diversification strategy based upon percentages looks like this:

30 percent of my money will be invested in stocks, 50 percent in bonds, and 20 percent in cash,
or

70 percent of my money is invested in stocks, 20 percent in bonds, and 10 percent in cash,
or
60 percent of my money is invested in stocks, 30 percent in bonds, and 10 percent in cash.

No single diversification strategy is right for everyone. Any of these strategies—or many others—could work for you. But you have to make a decision. You have to make a plan. One of the ways you can decide the diversification percentages is based upon your age. The closer you are to your retirement—stage three—the less in stocks you may want to have. So you may have 70 percent invested in stocks when you are in your thirties but may have 30 percent invested in stocks when you are in your seventies. Money invested in stocks has more volatility than money invested in bonds or cash. Volatility means the value of the investment moves up and down. One of the reasons you may have less money in stocks as you get older is to lower the risk of volatility to your investments. In a bear market, the value of your stock investments goes down. In a bull market, the value of your stock investments goes up. When you are in your thirties and have many years before you need the money you have invested for stage three, you don't have to worry about your investment going up and down. If the market does go down, you have time until the market moves up and grows again. If you are in your seventies, you don't have as much time to wait for the market to stabilize and grow again. That's why you may want to have less money in stocks as you get older.

Within each of these broad categories—stocks, bonds, and cash—you'll diversify further. Stocks need to be diversified into large, medium, and small growth stocks. Large, medium, and small refer to the size of the business you are investing in. Different-sized businesses do better in some economies than in others, so you want to have a mixture of stocks based upon size. Also, you should consider investing some money in two other categories of stocks. One category is value stocks. Very simply, when you invest in value stocks you are investing in businesses that are good companies, but for some reason the price of their stock is lower right now. The other category is international stocks. When you invest internationally, you are investing in other parts of the world. Since our economy is a world economy, these investments increase your diversification. Unless you're very knowledgeable or have a financial professional who can pick stocks and bonds for you, the best way to get good diversification may be by using several mutual funds rather than individual stocks and bonds. A mutual fund is a mixture of investments. It can be a mixture of different sizes of businesses—invested in stocks or in bonds or in both. It can be a mixture of many business all of one size—either in stocks or in bonds or in both. It can be a mixture of business in any part of the world—you just need to know where. Before you invest in a mutual fund, it is important that you understand what that fund's mixture is so you can make sure it fits into your diversification strategy—your percentages. Every mutual fund prospectus explains what kind of investments are in that particular fund. The prospectus booklet is available through your mutual fund company or your financial professional.

In your diversification strategy you will make a plan where you say, "I will put $$$$ amount each month into these three mutual funds based on the diversified percentages I have chosen." Then, once a year—at the same time every year—you readjust—*without emotion*—based on the percentages of your diversified plan.

You have learned to follow your diversified investment plan *without emotion*. Diversification of your invested money involves the same concept as the concept of balance in the different facets of your life—spiritual, emotional, physical, and financial. You learned about life balance in chapter 5. You learned that in order to make your life-planning really work you need the four facets to be in balance. You also learned how fear and greed can destroy this life balance. Diversification is a form of balance. This means the emotions of fear and greed can, if you let them, also destroy your diversified, balanced financial plan. You learned in chapter 5 that greed can convince you to chase returns and fear can convince you to run from the market. My advice is, "Stick to your diversified plan, even when you feel fear or greed." When you make decisions out of fear or greed, you always end up regretting those decisions. Stick to your plan.

A financial professional can help you set up your diversified investment plan. Get names of professionals from friends and colleagues. Then interview—by phone or in person—several of the professionals. Make sure the professional listens to your questions and answers them in a way you can understand. Ask for the professional's definition of diversification. And find out what it will cost to work with this professional.

Again, if you are unsure about how to get your diversification strategy started, find someone to work with who is knowledgable and skilled. And get going!

Dollar Cost Averaging: Investing Money Consistently

The second rule about invested money is that, as an investor, you need to understand the concept of dollar cost averaging. This term means that you will decide how much money you are going to invest each year—the dollar cost—and average it out over the year. In other words, you will invest this money each paycheck or each month—month after month after month—consistently over time. Let's say you decide to invest $3600 a year. By dollar cost averaging, you would then invest $300 each month of the year to get to your $3600. You invest the $300 every month—not worrying about whether the price is high or low—just get the money invested. Over time, the price of the investment will average out if you just keep investing the money consistently.

The primary reason people don't have enough money for stage three is that they haven't invested *enough* money, *long* enough, and *consistently* enough in a diversified portfolio.

Remember, we'll always have recessionary markets and we'll always have growth markets. These markets simply alternate. Your job is to start investing at as young an age as possible and to keep investing—with a strategy of diversification—consistently over time. That's the key to wealth building. That's the key to a financially successful stage three.

Principle of Money #3: Minimize Your Debt

Unmanaged and inefficient debt devastates financial life-planning. Unmanaged and inefficient debt destroys wealth building. That's the truth. If you want to make your money life successful now and in the future, you must get a handle on debt. This, of course, is dependent on *spending less than you earn* (principle #1). If you don't *minimize debt* (principle #3), you won't be able to *invest the difference* (principle #2). These three principles work together.

Debt insidiously destroys financial life-planning because it means that you are paying a bill *this* month for what you did *last* month. Debt consumes the money *this* month that you were supposed to use for *this* month's expenses. If you're using *this* month's money for what you did *last* month, where will you get the money to pay for *this* month's bills? And where will you get the money for investing for the future? So, let's look at strategies for managing your debt.

First, minimize your debt. By getting a handle on your spending (principle #1) you can get a handle on your debt.

Second, make the debt you have right now more efficient. More efficient debt means that you are paying the lowest interest possible on that debt. The lower your interest, the more your payment will go to reduce the principle (the amount you owe). More efficient debt also means, if possible, restructuring the debt so the interest that you're paying on that debt is tax-deductible. One means of restructuring your debt is to use equity from your home. Home equity debt is usually the most efficient debt because it is usually borrowed at lower interest rates and the interest is tax deductible. Be careful, however. If you use your home equity to pay off your credit cards, make sure you get rid of those cards so that you don't start to use them again. If you don't get rid of those cards, you probably will have a home equity debt and also a growing debt on your credit cards.

Third, pay off the debt. Get out of debt! Look at the budget you calculated earlier in this chapter. Look at how much money you would have every month if you didn't have debt payments. If you didn't have any debt payments, you would have all the money that you earned *this* month to pay for *this* month's expenses and to invest for the future. Your life would feel better and it will work better financially.

Principle #4: Plan for Catastrophes

Make planning for catastrophes a part of your financial life-planning. If catastrophes aren't anticipated, your budget won't work, your investing plan will fall apart, and you probably will increase debt rather than minimize debt.

To make all the principles of money work, principle #4 must be included in your plan.

Planning for Catastrophes Takes Two Forms

Emergency savings is your "God forbid" account.

First, you need cash in case something really bad happens. You already learned, in the spending principle (principle #1), that cash savings for an emergency is absolutely critical to making your life-plan work. Make sure every paycheck or every month you put money into a savings account and then *leave it there*. You don't want to have the revolving door syndrome with your savings account. You put it in, then you take it out—then you put it in, then you take it out.

Cash in the bank is the foundation of good financial life-planning. Let the money stay in the bank. The rule of emergency savings is that you can't take it out for anything that's just part of life—like car repair or vacation, like a root canal or property taxes, like the mortgage or the vet bill. You'll have to find the money for those expenses somewhere else—in some other savings account. Your emergency savings account is absolutely untouchable unless you are laid off from work or you are disabled. Emergency savings is for a catastrophe. I call this savings the "God forbid" account. Put your money into this account and leave it alone. This emergency savings will help you feel safe in case something really bad happens in your life.

Insurance Protection for Catastrophes

Second, as you plan for catastrophes, you must consider insurance for protection. You probably already know you need good health insurance—a medical condition without insurance could devastate your entire financial plan. You also know you need good car insurance in case of a car accident. You need life insurance if you have dependents whose lives will be financially impacted upon your death. If you don't know about the importance of these three kinds of insurance, talk to your financial professional to get more information.

The two insurances you may not know you need are disability insurance and long-term care insurance. Both are important to planning for catastrophic events.

Disability insurance replaces part of your income if you can't work. You need disability insurance if you need your income. It's really that clear and simple. If you can't work and you need your income, none of these principles of money will work without disability insurance. The budget won't work. You'll probably end up not only stopping your investment plan but also probably cashing out and spending the money you have already invested for the future to pay for bills today. Disability insurance is critical to this principle.

Long-term care insurance protects you in case you become ill and need assistance for care. After age sixty-five—during stage three—you have over a 70 percent chance of needing some form of care. Long-term care insurance pays for all or part of the costs of that care. A good long-term care policy covers three levels of care: in-home health care, out-of-the-home assisted-living care, and nursing-home care. Paying for any of these levels of care—on your own without insurance—could devastate your life-planning. In addition, if you are married, any of these levels of care needed by one member of the marriage could decimate your invested money, leaving the surviving spouse with little or no invested money for the future.

If you want your life-planning to be successful, make sure that planning for catastrophes is part of it.

In the last three chapters you've gathered information about yourself—what *you* want and need to feel good about your life. You've gathered information about your *work*—paid and unpaid work. And you've gathered information about *money*—and the four principles of money:

Principle #1: Spend less than you earn.

Principle #2: Invest the difference.

Principle #3: Minimize your debt.

Principle #4: Plan for catastrophes.

Now you're ready to put all the information and skills together as you create a life-plan for retirement.

CHAPTER TEN

How Long Does "Old" Last?

Courage is not the lack of fear but being willing to act anyway.
—Mark Twain

According to the American Savings Educational Council (2001) most people spend more time planning a two-week vacation than planning for a possible 30-year retirement.

When we avoid planning for the last stage of our lives—our retirement—we are making two major mistakes.

Mistake #1: *Hoping* That Retirement Will Work Rather Than *Planning* for Retirement

Seventy percent of Americans say that they are confident they'll have enough money to live comfortably in retirement. But one-half of all workers have saved less than $50,000, and 15 percent of workers have saved zero. According to the Library of Congress research, 55 percent of people ages forty-five to fifty-four have no retirement investments. One-half of those with investments have less than $20,000.

This is not planning. This is, at best, hope and, at worst, denial. These statistics tell us that many Americans haven't made a decision to make the financial facet of stage three of their lives really work. They haven't started planning. Oh, they may be putting a little money away—*hoping* it will be enough. But they don't really know.

"Come on, Patricia!" I cajoled my fifty-two-year-old client. "What are you waiting for? You have to start preparing for the third stage of your life. It's coming whether you're ready or not! If you don't plan, you will have so few choices. Do you realize that you won't even be able to afford your antidepressants when you retire unless you start investing some significant money—now? And," I said with a smile, "you're really going to need those antidepressants if you'll be living only on Social Security income."

Planning with Hope Works!

Hoping, all by itself, doesn't work. But planning with hope does work. Planning liberates you. When you plan, there can be no denial. That's liberating! Living without denial is difficult and takes courage, but the rewards are great. Living without denial gives you freedom—freedom to creatively write the next chapter in your life. You won't be just hoping for the best.

Planning allows you to focus on what you can control, not the end result. Planning allows you to get clear about what you want to create—spiritually, emotionally, physically, financially—and how you're going to do it. We all know that in this process you have no control of the outcome. Planning for retirement is really no different from planning for a new baby, or planning for a new job, or planning to buy a house.

Before you make a big life change, *any* big life change, you first prepare yourself emotionally. You've already done that in this book. Also, before any big life change, you spend time gathering information so you can be as prepared as possible for that change. You've done that too. You've gathered information about yourself, your work, and your money. The final step is for you to develop a plan about how and when you'll take this big life-changing step for which you've been preparing.

There is an old saying, "If you want to make God laugh, make a plan." Even after all of your preparation, you still can't know how everything will turn out. This is true for any kind of planning. You can't know in advance how successful you will be as a parent when you have that new baby. You can't know if the new job will work long-term when you accept that new position. You can't know if you'll really like that new house and neighborhood when you buy that house. And, of course, you can't know what the third stage of your life will actually bring until you get there. Nonetheless, for any chance of success, planning is essential.

Many people *hoping* for a good retirement say, "Maybe I'll win the lottery." That is 100 percent hope with 100 percent denial thrown in. And obviously, it isn't a plan. If you don't plan and aren't willing to do what you need to do to make the plan work, you're gambling with your life. You're gambling with the third stage of your life. You deserve better.

Whenever you make a big life change, you have to expect that all will work out, and you must also accept that you have no real control over the outcome. The only control you have is control of the process of planning. It's your life! You *get to* and you *need to* plan for it!

Mistake #2: Planning Too Simplistically for Retirement

"Well, Ruth," John said in a resigned voice, "I figure if Liz and I can get a few good years after we both retire, we'll be lucky. If we can do a little travel and not have any major medical problems, then we'll have to take whatever the Fates give us and do the best with what we get." Then he added pensively, "I sure hope I get a few good years before I have to go into a nursing home."

John just made the second major mistake most people make when planning for retirement. He's thinking too simplistically about the last third of his life.

Stage three of your life will be just as complex and multidimensional as stages one and two. And stage three will probably be just as long or longer. In chapter 6 you learned that most people view retirement—stage three—in two phases. The first phase is about freedom—freedom from work you don't like, freedom from people you don't like, and freedom from a schedule you don't like. In looking forward to retirement, most people hope they get a few good years of freedom before moving into the second phase of retirement, which is when they expect something bad to happen—like getting sick, breaking a hip, or running out of money. I find that my clients don't want to talk at all about the second phase, but if they do, they talk passively about their life after those first few good years. They say things like, "Well, whatever happens, I sure hope I can keep my health." Or, "I sure hope I'll have enough money and be able to keep my independence." Or, "I hope I never have to go into a nursing home." Mostly people talk about that part of their lives with a sigh. They're simply resigned to and a little worried about that second phase of stage three.

You already know that hope without planning doesn't work.

You know that a simplistic, two-phase view of the last third of your life doesn't work either. When you plan for the third stage of your life you have to be willing to plan for *all* of it—for all of its complexities and all of its years. For some of us this third stage will last more than 30 years. Thirty full, frustrating, fun, fabulous, and feisty years!

To avoid the second major mistake that people make as they look forward to stage three, you already know that you must plan in a way that accounts for all facets of your life—spiritual, emotional, physical, and financial.

You also already know that life-planning is about making your life work in all three life stages:

Stage one—birth to twenty-nine years old
Stage two—thirty to fifty-nine years old
Stage three—sixty to ninety years old and beyond

For your life-planning to work and work well, you must be willing to plan for different time frames in each of the three stages. That means you need to divide each of the three stages into thirds—so when you're done, you'll have three time frames in each of the three stages. You have to do this because 30 years—which is the projected length of stage three—is too long and complex to deal with in one big lump. Just as stages one and two of your life are multidimensional, so too will be stage three. Each time frame within each stage has different problems to solve. The solutions require different strategies than in the time frame before it. For example, in stage one, you wouldn't use the same strategy for a two-year-old (which falls in the first time frame in stage one) as you would for yourself at age twenty-two (which falls in the second time frame in stage one). A two-year-old needs a time out chair, potty training, and someone to read to him or her. A twenty-two year-old needs to look for a job, understand the 401(k) options at a new job, or deal with an increase in car insurance because of speeding tickets. The problems of a particular age require different strategies.

Yet when I hear people talk about getting old, they talk in terms of one strategy. They retire. They're done with work. The pressure is gone. They hope to have some fun until they can't anymore. They hope to take care of themselves until they can't anymore. They hope for the best. Then they die.

This strategy is far too simplistic. We are talking about a possible time period of 30 years or more. Yet, as a result of the finish-line model of retirement, we have accepted this simplistic strategy as we life-plan for stage three. It doesn't work. Your life has to work, remember? This includes the last third of your life.

Using age as a marker, divide each of the three stages into three time frames. The division by age is arbitrary so you can adjust these time frames as you choose.

Stage one: **First time frame**—Birth to age ten (dependent)
Second time frame—Ages eleven (prepuberty) to twenty-two (end of school years)
Third time frame—Ages twenty-three to twenty-nine (young adult and independent)

Stage two: **First time frame**—Ages thirty to thirty-nine (the thirties)

             Second time frame—Ages forty to forty-nine (the forties)

             Third time frame—Ages fifty to fifty-nine (the fifties)

Stage three: **First time frame**—Ages sixty to sixty-nine (the sixties)

             Second time frame—Ages seventy to seventy-nine (the seventies)

             Third time frame—Ages eighty to ninety and beyond (the eighties)

Look back at chapter 2 to see how you described stage one. Being six years old is very different from being thirteen, which is very different from being twenty-eight. Do you see how the challenges are different for the different ages? And because of that, the strategies to meet those challenges are different.

The same is true for stage two. What were your challenges in your thirties (the first time frame in stage two)? How were those challenges different from the challenges in your forties (the second time frame in stage two)? And how were those challenges different from the challenges of your fifties (the third time frame in stage two)? Each decade is unique, but *you* are the constant in all the decades. And the circumstances of your life—how you spend your time and your relationships—are different in each time frame.

Stage three is no different. The sixties are very different from the seventies, and the seventies different from the eighties. Again, each time frame has different challenges, and these challenges need different strategies as you life-plan.

The focus in this book is to help you to plan for stage three of your life. Because of this focus, we won't spend time strategizing options for stages one and two. The next three chapters represent the three time frames of stage three—your retirement. In chapter 11 you'll work with ages sixty to sixty-nine. In chapter 12 you'll work with ages seventy to seventy-nine. And in chapter 13 you'll work with ages eighty to ninety and older.

Whatever age you are now, work through the chapters as if you are *that specific age* in *that specific time frame.* This means that if you are forty-five years old, in the second time frame, you will need to *pretend* that you are in your seventies when you answer the questions. By actually *pretending* you are in that time frame, you will be able to get a better feel for what that time frame will be like. You will be able to start to develop your brain a very clear picture of all the challenges you'll face when you are in that time frame along with specific strategies for meeting those challenges. You also need to see the unending possibilities for this third stage of your life spiritually, emotionally, physically, and financially.

CHAPTER ELEVEN

Just a Youngster
Your Sixties

Retirement at sixty-five is ridiculous!
When I was sixty-five, I still had pimples.
—*George Burns*

It's time! It's finally time for you to develop a focused plan for stage three. We'll start with the first time frame—that is, the sixties.

The third stage of your life can give you incredible satisfaction if you purposefully work to create the groundwork for that satisfaction. Your retirement years can truly be your "golden years" if you decide to make them golden. You have learned that this won't happen without thoughtful planning.

Again, as you learned in the last chapter, even if you aren't sixty years old, it's important that you work through this chapter as if you were sixty so you can "practice" being in this stage, this decade. "But," you say, "I'm only forty-nine years old. Why should I 'practice' being in my sixties?" The answer is this: "Practicing" will help you get a much clearer picture of what you need to do to plan for this time of your life. This planning will work better because you've actually "tried-on" this stage of your life and this stage feels real to you. When this stage feels real to you, your planning will always be more effective.

A Vision of Your Future Is the Beginning of Successful Life-Planning

The beginning of any creative life-planning is to form a picture of what you want your life to look like. To form this picture, you create a vision statement, as we discussed in chapter 6. A vision statement is critical because it gives your brain a picture—in words—of what you're working to create in your life. In chapter 6 you wrote a vision statement for *all* of stage three of your life. Mine said, "When I'm seventy-nine, I want to be feisty, strong-willed, loved, and lovable. I want to be needed by someone. I want enough money so I will have choices of where I live and be able to pay for care if I need it. And I want to wear really big hats."

That was mine. What was yours?

Now you need to write another vision statement. This one will be a specific statement for just the first time frame of stage three—your sixties. It will include what you want to accomplish—what you want your life to look like and what you want your life to feel like—for this specific decade. Make sure this vision statement includes, in some way, all four facets of life: spiritual, emotional, physical, and financial.

My vision statement for this decade is: "I want to be physically active. I want travel to be a big part of my sixties. I want to hike the canyons of Zion Park and the trails of Lake Louise—at least twice. I will continue writing and teaching with larger breaks for the travel. I will keep accumulating money for the future. I will keep enjoying my family—and my partner, Don—as I continue to grow more feisty and keep wearing my big hats."

So, what's yours? Ask yourself:

Keeping in mind the four facets of life, what is my vision for the first time frame of stage three of my life?

Write down your vision statement.

Now, keeping your vision in mind, let's get specific. Again, if you're not sixty, think like you're sixty as you work through this chapter.

Money for retirement is the primary worry that pre-retirees have about stage three. You have learned that the majority of people will not have enough money to exercise the old retirement model. To help you determine what your retirement model will be, let's deal with money first.

"How much money will I need to retire?" is a question you may have asked; most people ask that question. The question usually means, "Do I have enough money to exercise the old model of retirement?"

Everyone wants an answer to this question—an attainable magical number—so we can retire without worry. As we discussed earlier, this question is absolutely impossible to answer. Anyone who gives you a definitive answer to this question needs to be questioned. Even the most astute financial professional can't accurately calculate with absolute certainty how much money you will need for 30 years. There are too many variables in the economy and too many variables in your life.

The other way people try to answer this question is by trying to figure out what percentage of your current income you will need in order to be able to retire. Some financial professionals may tell you that you will need 60 percent of your current income, or maybe even 75 percent of your current income. Percentages won't help much. They may, on the one hand, create a false sense of security or, on the other hand, unnecessary fear.

"I don't know what to do now," my client Chris explained. "I retired two years ago from a healthy six-figure job on the advice of my financial advisor. It was a job that had a lot of pressure, but it paid me well. And, even though I've lived well, I have always been good at saving money. So I had put away a significant amount. Two years ago I was fifty years old and had enough money to get out of the rat race and not worry about money ever again. I calculated that if I could live on about 75 percent of my pre-retirement income, I would be all right. I've been traveling and writing. It's been good. That is, until my financial advisor called me last week and told me he thought I needed to get another job—I was running out of money! I couldn't believe my ears. Two years is the shortest retirement I've ever heard of. But between the stock market going down, some higher than expected health care expenses, and higher than expected travel costs, I'm in trouble. I have to get a job. I should've just stayed in my old job. It would have been easier."

Chris' life style cost significantly more than he was financially prepared to pay. Between that and retiring at the beginning of a bear market, Chris' retirement plans fell apart.

Like Chris, very few people will be able to put away enough money to live a good life for 30 or more years—without worry. That's the old finish-line model of retirement. Longevity outdates that model. You already know that. You don't want to do what Chris did and start running out of money. Actually, Chris is fortunate. He's young and has many job opportunities. It would have been a different story if this scenario had happened when he was in his seventies.

How can you know how much money you'll need? Here's the strategy, but remember, this strategy is for this first time frame of stage three *only*—your sixties. You will plan for the next retirement time frames—the next decades—in chapters 12 and 13.

In this first time frame of stage three, you still need to earn money. As much as you might not want to admit this, you know it's true. If you were your grandmother or grandfather, you might die in this decade. You would probably die before you ran out of money. But you're not them. You're planning to live twenty-five to thirty-five more years now that you've reached your sixties. Your paid-work life can't be over yet. To live long and well, you need to accumulate additional money during this decade so you can be financially safe when you're an eighty-year-old.

Stall the Use of Your Investments

The three time frames in stage three of your life have to work together. If you start using your 401(k) or 403(b) or other retirement plan money now, when you're sixty or sixty-five, you probably won't have enough money left when you're eighty. That's the truth. To make the next two time frames work—your seventies and eighties, and maybe even nineties—you have to be willing to not only stall the use of your current retirement investments but also actually continue adding to them. If you start using this money now, your money may run out before you do. Remember, the plan is, *you are going to live!*

So, in this first time frame, you need to keep earning income and keep accumulating money that will be used, if needed, in the next two time frames of stage three.

Quit Your Job but Don't Retire

"But Ruth," Tom protested, "I have to get out of this job. I have to! If I can't retire in less than two years, I think this job will kill me."

"Relax, Tom," I told him. "Paid work is for the purpose of earning money. Work was never meant to kill anyone."

The solution for Tom, and maybe for you if you feel like Tom, is to quit the current job but don't retire. In other words, Tom needs to find another job. He needs to take this next year and a half to find a new career while he keeps his present job. He needs to find a job that he can do, that he wants to do, and one that will pay him money. It may not pay as much money as he's earning right now. That's okay. But he needs to earn *enough* money to pay for his expenses in this decade and still be able to invest—even just a little—for the next two time frames in stage three.

"Maybe I'll start my own consulting business," Tom responded. "I've always wanted to have my own business. I could start the business now. Begin marketing. And I may be positioned perfectly in a year or so to go into it full-time by the time I'm sixty. You know, Ruth, this could be the best thing that ever happened to me. I may even make more money in my sixties than in my fifties."

By the way, did you hear how Tom just used the skill of resiliency—What if . . . ? Then what . . . ?—to get to a solution?

Ideally, your paid-work, in this first time frame of stage three, needs to be more of what your true work is—what you'd really like to do. Your work for money needs to be the work that feeds you—not drains you. Remember what you learned about yourself and your work in chapter 8? If you're willing to use this stage three life-planning as an opportunity to find paid-work that is more in balance for you—spiritually, emotionally, and physically—what would you do? Really think about it! Take this seriously. What would you—could you—do?

Could you work part-time in your current job and do something else for 10 to 20 hours per week that may not pay as much but would be more fulfilling?

"I know what I could do," Kim said in an excited tone. "I'm a nurse. I've worked nights at the hospital so I could be around during the day for the kids. By the way, don't ask me when I sleep. Night work at the hospital pays the best, and we needed the money. That's the other reason I've done it. But, if I didn't need to earn as much money, what I would really like to do is work at a clinic as a pediatric nurse. At a clinic you can establish relationships with patients. I would like that. And physically, it would be easier. Clinics pay less but, I think, we would need less money. I could work days and have a more normal social life. If we can make the budget work, and I think we can, eventually I could go down to four days a week and maybe we could go to the cabin—which will be paid for by then—for three-day weekends. Now that sounds like fun!"

Kim found a possible solution.

You can find one, too.

Remember the information you gathered in chapter 8 about your work? What work do you like? What work don't you like?

What work feels useful to you? What work is satisfying to you? What work feels productive to you? This is the time to use the information that you gathered about your work. Ask yourself:

What work could I do that would be in balance for me spiritually, emotionally, and physically—and still earn money?

If you're stuck, get help. Brainstorm with a friend—someone who really knows you well enough to help you generate ideas. Or, this might be the time to get the help of an expert—a career or vocational counselor. Experts have knowledge that you don't have. You may have a general idea of what you could do, but an expert can really help you get specific about work. An expert in careers can help you get moving and keep a balance between realism and creativity—between how you can earn enough to pay your bills and how you can work at something you really like. If you're stuck or unsure of yourself, set up an appointment and get some vocational testing and analysis. Bring the information that you gathered in chapter 8 with you to that appointment. Then, in that appointment, get help answering this question:

What could I do for money that would be closer to the work that feeds me—not drains me? That stimulates me—not dulls my brain? That makes me feel more satisfied instead of frustrated?

This is an opportunity to change your paid-work life. This is an opportunity to make your whole life better. It's a wonderfully creative opportunity—if you take it.

If you choose, instead, to be rigid because you don't want to "have to work" anymore, you may want to go back to chapter 4 and read about resiliency.

Or, if making this kind of life-work change just plain scares you, you may want to reread chapter 3 about healthy defiance.

Or, if you just want to wait and see what will happen, you may want to go back to chapter 5 and read about denial and fear.

Use this as an opportunity to make a change in your life that will enhance your life in all facets—spiritually, emotionally, physically and, of course, financially. Stretch yourself. Come up with an idea. Ask yourself:

What could my paid work be when I am sixty years old— for about a decade in the first time frame of stage three?

You did it! You came up with an idea. At least I hope you did. Congratulations on getting creative about your paid-work life.

Now you have to be able to answer the question, "How much money do I need to earn in this new job of mine during this first decade of stage three?" To answer this question, you will need to calculate how much money you will need so you can pay your bills and expenses *while* you are still putting away at least a little money for the second and third time frames of stage three.

The easiest way to calculate your financial needs during this time frame, and I believe the most accurate way, is to do your calculations based on cash flow planning. I'll take you through the simple but clear steps to do this.

What Are My Expenses?

You need to know the total cost of your monthly expenses. Start with the number you calculated in chapter 9. Will any of those bills and expenses *no longer* be part of your financial life when you're in your sixties? Maybe your house will be paid off by then. Or your cabin. Or the student loan for your child or maybe even the student loan for yourself. What is the total for the expenses or bills that *will not* exist during your sixties? Subtract that number from the budgeting number you calculated in chapter 9. You should now have a number that represents your real bills and expenses for your sixties.

What is my new budgeting total?

It's fun to see bills that have been on your to-pay list disappear. However, now you need to look for any *new expenses* that were not part of your life in your fifties but may be part of your life in your sixties. These expenses may include increased travel expenses since you may have more time. Or presents for the grandkids. Or education costs such as that watercolor or woodworking class you've always wanted to take. Or increased medical costs. Or the cost of the career counselor. Add these expenses to your new budgeting total.

So, this is what you've done so far:

Present-day expense total (from chapter 9)

Subtract—expenses that will *not* be part of my life

Add—expenses that *will* be part of my life

What is that new budgeting number?

This new budgeting number is the amount of money you need for expenses and bills. It is the amount of money you will need *after* you've paid all your income taxes. In other words, it's the net amount you need to earn. To figure out the gross amount—the amount you need to earn which includes the income taxes you will need to pay—check with your financial professional who can give you the most accurate calculation based on your tax bracket and deductions. Or, you can make a rough estimate by adding about a third to your budgeting needs to include taxes. For example, if you need $2000 per month to pay your bills and expenses, you'll need to earn approximately $2700 per month if you include taxes. If you need $6000 per month for your budget, you'll need approximately $8000 per month to pay for expenses and taxes.

How much—in total—including taxes, do I need to earn each month during my sixties?

Benefits

One final part of your money calculation involves benefits. There are two kinds of benefits.

The first is your retirement benefit. For most people these retirement benefits are defined-contribution plans such as 401(k) or 403(b) plans if you work for a company (profit or nonprofit). Or it could be a SIMPLE plan or a SEP-IRA if you work for yourself. As you've already learned, you'll need to continue to contribute—at least a little money—to a defined contribution plan. It may not be nearly as much as you have been contributing, but you may still need to contribute even a small amount of money for the next decade. In chapter 9, you set the diversification percentages for your invested money (stocks, bonds, and cash). Also in chapter 9, you learned that you would probably make some adjustments in those percentages as you got older. In this first time frame of stage three, you will probably want to adjust those percentages. You may still want to invest a small amount of money in stocks, but, because of your age, you'll probably want to significantly increase the amount you invest in bonds and cash.

This would be a good time to meet with your financial professional and ask for help in resetting the diversification percentages, not just for the new money you are still accumulating but also for the money you have already accumulated.

Ask yourself:

What are my new diversification percentages (in stocks, bonds, and cash) for the money I am still accumulating for use in the second and third time frames of stage three?

Based on how I earn my income, what investment structure will I use for this time frame—401(k), 403(b), SEP-IRA, SIMPLE, Roth IRA, or regular IRA?

Here's the cash flow question:

How much money will I put away each month—now in my sixties—for the last two time frames in stage three?

How much do I need to add to my monthly budget so I can do this?

The second benefit category you need to consider is your insurance. What are the insurance coverages for which you still need to budget—such as health, dental, disability, and long-term care insurance? Are any of these paid—all or in part—through your work? Don't forget, your disability insurance will probably end at age sixty-five, but it's probably worth carrying until then. Now the big question:

How much will these benefits cost me?

How will I pay for the continuation of these benefits?

Add this number to the budgeting total. Your worksheet will look like this:

Present-day expense total (from chapter 9)

Subtract—Expenses that will *not* be part of my life (in my sixties)

Add—New expenses that *will* be part of my life (in my sixties)

Add— Income taxes

*Add—*Benefits

You did it! All the money pieces are now in place. You've figured out the monthly expense budget. You've added taxes. You've added the cost of benefits.

Now we need a final total.

What is the total amount of money I need to earn—per month, during my sixties—to cover my bills and expenses, my taxes, and my benefits?

If you want to be more accurate and factor in inflation, check with your financial professional. Be sure to factor inflation in both increased expenses and increased income—or you will scare yourself.

What Are My Sources of Income?

What sources of income do you have during your sixties that aren't paid-work income? For example, your Social Security income may start sometime during this decade. You may have a fixed-benefit pension from a former job. You may have an annuity that will start sometime during this decade.

Remember, we are *not* talking about the money you've invested in regular or Roth IRAs, SEP-IRAs, SIMPLE plans, 401(k)s, 403(b)s, and deferred compensation plans. This money is your defined-contribution retirement money—your flexible retirement money. You are *not only* leaving it alone, but you are still investing a little money into one of these defined-contribution plans. In other words, you are still growing money for the last two decades of your retirement. Leave this money alone—you're going to need it later.

Your question to yourself is:

What sources of income do I have that may start some-time during my sixties?

How much income will that bring to me and when?

Subtract that income amount from your expense total that you just calculated.

What is the new total number?

This new total is the amount of money you'll need to earn each month at your work. This amount may not remain constant during your sixties. For example, you may need to earn more money in your early sixties and less in your middle sixties when your Social Security income starts.

Think of this time frame as a kind of creative puzzle—you're trying to fit the income pieces with the expense pieces in a way that will work.

Remember the skill of resiliency? You say to yourself, "I will need to earn *this* amount of money from sixty to sixty-five. *How will I do that?*"

Then from sixty-five to sixty-nine, you say to yourself, "I will need to earn *this* amount of money—probably less. *How will I do that?*"

Keep working the puzzle. If you can't figure out how to earn this much money doing what you said you want to do during this decade, then go back and work with your expenses again. Is there any expense that could be reduced or eliminated during this decade—any compromise you could make in your life style? The language of compromise is, "I'd rather not do that. But if I did, I could live with it and be all right." Is there any way to reduce your expenses? Keep working the puzzle. One part of the puzzle is your work income, the other is your expenses. During this time frame, how can you make the money part of your life—income and expenses—work for you?

Life-Planning Involves More Than Money

So you've figured out a plan for the money part of the first time frame of stage three—the time frame in which you may begin to phase-in your retirement. However, you've also learned that life-planning involves more than money. Money is essential. But without planning for the emotional, spiritual, and physical aspects of your life, money won't really matter either.

In chapter 7 you answered the question, "Who am I?" In that chapter you explored what you enjoy, what stimulates you, who you like to be with, and where you like to live. You also asked yourself, "What do I want to make sure I have accomplished before I die?" You gathered information about yourself and your life that you'll now use as you continue your life-plan.

Using that information, answer some questions about this specific time frame—your sixties. You may never have asked yourself some of these questions. Some answers may be difficult, even painful, to think about. Take your time. This is your life.

When I'm sixty years old, where will I live? Will the place I call home give me the most emotional satisfaction? Will I be able to afford to live there? Will that place support any physical needs that I may have?

When I am sixty years old, whom will I live with? And why?

Who else will I want to include in my life? What other relationships do I want in my life?

Some friends of mine started a routine when they were in their early sixties. They made arrangements with their son and his wife so that every Friday their only granddaughter spent the day with them rather than at her day care. They both made arrangements at their work to take Fridays off—which they could now afford to do. It lowered the child care costs for the parents.

And the granddaughter loved being with her "Boppa" and "Gramma."

What will I include in my life that will stimulate my thinking? What will I study? Read? Experience?

What will I include in my life that will stimulate me emotionally? That will create pleasure in my life? Anticipation? That will make me feel good about myself? That makes me happy?

What will I do to take care of my physical body? Exercise? Nutrition? Stress reduction? Physical play? Good medical care?

"Have you ever heard of Pilates?" Joan asked as she entered my office. Without waiting for a reply she continued. "You wouldn't believe all the ways my body can stretch. And bend. I decided if I was going to have movable joints in my seventies that I'd better start moving them in my sixties! And I'm doing it with a group of women," she added, "so it's fun too."

What will my work be that is *not* for income? What will I do to make me feel needed, to know that I am adding back to the world—both my world of family and friends and the greater world?

How will I create my legacy? What will determine how I want to be remembered, to know that my being here mattered?

Get clear. Stay creative. Be purposeful.
This is your life. Make it work.
You can, you know.

CHAPTER TWELVE

So This Is Midlife!
Your Seventies

The longer I live the more beautiful life becomes.
—Frank Lloyd Wright

Y ou're still here! Congratulations! As a seventy-year-old you're in the midlife time frame of stage three. No, it's not time for a midlife crisis—that's not what this chapter is about. This chapter is about purposefully planning your seventies—spiritually, emotionally, physically, and financially. Just as the decades of stage one (birth to twenty-nine) and stage two (thirty to fifty-nine) of your life had similarities and differences, so too will the decades of stage three.

As you learned in the last chapter, even if you aren't seventy years old right now, it's important that you pretend that you are seventy years old as you work through this chapter. Even if you are still forty-nine years old—or whatever age you were when you began reading this book—you will want to practice being in your seventies. This practice will help you plan for your seventies in a way that will actually work. So answer each question in this chapter as if you were actually seventy years old.

As a seventy year old, you're older. We know that. If you're not sure, look at a picture of yourself ten years ago. Yes, you're older—physically. You're also wiser than you were even a decade ago. You've been developing wisdom through your emotional and spiritual growth. You've stayed flexible and hopeful. Remember resiliency? You've avoided fear and greed. You've learned to be healthily defiant in creating a life that works. You are purposefully creating your life and will continue to do so.

A Vision Creates a Picture for Your Brain of What You Want

So, once again, we'll begin with a vision statement. You want to create a specific picture of this time frame—your seventies. Again, you need to give your brain a picture—in words—of what you want your life to be for this time period. If you don't, the only picture your brain will have is what you saw—in your relatives and friends—of what the seventies looked like. If you want your life to be different—in full or in part—you need to give your brain a different picture so it can create something new.

My vision statement for my seventies is: "I will continue to travel and hike in the national parks with my partner. I will continue a small, part-time educational/consulting business. I will continue to teach and write. Maybe I'll even write my first mystery novel! I will make time for more volunteering and for family. And I will take much more time for reading. I will continue to be feisty and wear my big hats."

Now it's your turn. Ask yourself:

What is my vision for this decade—my seventies? What do I want to create spiritually, emotionally, physically, and financially? What do I want my seventies to look like and feel like?

Write down your vision statement.

Keeping your vision statement in mind, let's get to specific planning, beginning with money.

Protect the Golden Goose

Until now, you've been earning income and growing your investments. The safest financial strategy for the seventies is quite simple: You can consume the golden egg, but you don't kill the golden goose. Your principal—which is all the money you've accumulated so far—is the golden goose. All the interest and dividends you'll earn on this money—from now on—is the golden egg. This means you can spend the interest and dividends from your retirement nest egg, but, as much as possible while you are in your seventies, don't touch the principal. Not yet. You need to protect as much of the principal as possible for the third time frame in stage three—ages eighty to ninety and beyond. If you start spending significant principal now, you'll leave yourself too vulnerable for your eighties. You don't want to do that to yourself.

The most common planning strategy is to withdraw, year after year, 5 percent of your money—the value of your portfolio. It doesn't work, however, to take 5 percent out of your portfolio when this country is in a bear market and the returns on your investments are negative. Taking 5 percent of the value of the portfolio when the market is negative will take too much money out of your portfolio. The value will go down too far, too fast. If most retirees told the truth, they would tell you that when our country is in a bull market, they take out much more than the 5 percent because they see that their money is growing faster than 5 percent and they want to spend more. Based upon what I've seen in several bull markets, most retirees aren't able to avoid greed and they just keep taking out amounts larger than their planning anticipated.

Using dividends and interest as the spending amount is a solid strategy for your seventies and helps you manage your greed (bull markets) and your fear (bear markets). Since stage three could last 25 to 35 years—in which time period there will probably be several alternating bull and bear markets—this strategy helps to manage these emotions.

Using dividends and interest as the spending amount also means that you will probably want to talk with a financial professional while in your early sixties and begin to develop a strategy for your specific investments so you will have enough interest and dividend income for your seventies.

We'll get more specific with this strategy later in this chapter.

What Are My Sources of Income?

During this decade, you'll choose to work if you want additional income. You'll choose to work for income if your work stimulates you or makes you feel useful.

Once after I gave a speech, a woman from the audience came up and introduced herself. When she found out I was writing this book she said, "I was very smart, Ruth, when I picked a career many years ago. Oh, I know my body doesn't work so well. I have a heck of a time with my knees, which is why I use this cane. But I want you to know," she said, tapping the side of her head with her index finger, "that I'm still in great shape up here. In fact, I'm even better than I used to be. As a psychologist, my clients are still paying me for what I know up here." Again, she tapped the side of her head and continued with pride. "And I know a lot. I'm still earning income. The money I earn pays for all of my travel. Never thought I'd have so much fun in my late seventies." She looked around and noticed the number of individuals who were waiting to speak to me. "Well, if we had more time, Ruth, I could tell you my travel tales. I truly am having the time of my life, even with these knees of mine," she said with a smile as she walked away.

Think carefully and ask yourself:

Will I be earning any income during all or part of this decade (my seventies)?

If I will, how will I earn this income—what will I be doing?

Where?

How much do I think I will earn?

_____

Now, to summarize, ask yourself:

_____

During my seventies, what are all the sources of income I have that will come to me on a regular basis—monthly, quarterly, or annually?

On a *monthly* basis, during my seventies, what is the *average* amount I will receive from these regular sources of income? What is that total?

What Are My Expenses?

Now you know the total of your regular income sources. The next step is to know how much you will need to pay your bills and expenses when you're in your seventies—the second time frame of stage three. To determine this figure, we'll use the same structure we used in chapter 11. Go back to chapter 11 to find your answer to this question:

_____

What was the total amount of money that I needed in my sixties to pay each month for my expenses and bills and my taxes and benefits?

In my seventies, will I have any expenses or bills that will *not* be part of my life that were part of my life in my sixties?

_____

One expense that you will not have is putting money into your retirement plan.

Or maybe your house is finally paid off. I remember meeting a new client in my office for the first time who told me he was seventy-four years old and was still working part-time as an accountant. During the course of the conversation he told me that he had just refinanced his house with a 30-year mortgage.

"So you're not planning on paying it off before you retire?" I asked.

"Well, you never know, Ruth. I may not retire for 30 years."

Are there any *new* expenses that need to be added for my seventies?

This is what you've done so far:

Present-day expense total

Subtract—Expenses that will *not* be part of my life in my seventies.

Add—*New* expenses or bills that haven't been part of my life *but will be for my seventies.*

What is that new expense budgeting number?

As in chapter 11, this amount does *not* include income taxes. To determine the gross amount—which is the amount you need to earn including the amount for paying your income taxes—check with your financial professional, who can give you the most accurate calculation based on your tax bracket and deductions. Or, if you just want to get a rough estimate, add about a third to your budgeting needs to include taxes. So if you need $3000 to pay for your monthly bills, add about $1000 for taxes. The gross amount will be $4000. Again, as in the last chapter, if you want to be very accurate, factor in inflation. Check with your financial professional. Be sure to accurately factor increased health costs, which may exceed broad market or regular inflation.

So, how much—in total—including taxes, do I need each month during my seventies?

Add to this total the amount that I have already figured for my benefits not covered by my income work.

What is the *total*—including bills and expenses, taxes, and benefits—that I will need each month to pay for my life in my seventies?

Subtract from that total the amount of money I'll receive from regular sources—my Social Security, fixed benefit retirement, income, or any annuities.

What amount of my monthly costs are still *not* covered? (In other words, how much is my monthly shortfall?)

This monthly shortfall is the amount of money you'll need to take from your defined-contribution retirement money—your 401(k), your 403(b), your SEP-IRA, your SIMPLE, your Roth IRA, or your regular IRA. It's time to begin to use part of the money you have been investing all these years. Until now, you've done a wonderful job of protecting these investments for the last years of your life. You've worked for income longer than you thought you would. You have made contributions to these plans longer than you thought you would. And now is the appropriate time to begin to use this money.

But you need to have a plan.

Using Your Money Wisely

As you learned at the beginning of this chapter—protect your principal. That principal is your golden goose. If you spend some of that principal, you'll begin to kill your golden goose. This means if you take out money from the principal which is supposed to earn money for you through interest and dividends, you will not have as much earned money. The more principal you spend, the less money you will have earning money for you. You will need this principal—your golden goose—for your eighties and nineties.

Because protecting your principal is the safest *financial* strategy to have money for your eighties and nineties, it doesn't mean it is the *life style* definition for your seventies. You may need to modify your definition of protecting principal for your eighties and nineties in order to have enough money for your life style in your seventies. You may decide that the bonds, stocks, and mutual funds are your golden goose for your eighties and nineties, and you will spend only the interest and dividends from these investments. Then you may decide that your certificates of deposit, your money markets, and your treasuries (government bonds) can be used—in total, including both principal and interest—both the golden goose and the golden egg—for your seventies.

But you will have to decide.

In order to decide, you need more information about your current investments and how much they are earning in interest and dividends.

When you were in your sixties, you, as we noted earlier in this chapter, changed the investment strategy for your money. You probably got some advice from a financial professional in preparation for your seventies and decided to invest more money in cash and bonds than you had in stages one and two of your life. You still have money invested in stock, but you have more in cash and bonds.

So now, you ask yourself, what do I have?

Make a list of all the stock and stock mutual funds you have. Which of these investments pay dividends? How much have they been paying on the average? You'll now make arrangements to receive these dividends in cash, rather than reinvesting them. Your mutual fund company can help with this. Or you can get help from your financial professional.

Make a list of all the bonds and bond funds you have. How much in interest have these bonds and bond funds been paying on the average? Make arrangements to receive this interest in cash, rather than reinvesting it. Again, your mutual fund company or financial professional can help you do this.

Make a list of where your cash is. Is it in a money market fund, a certificate of deposit, a treasury? How much interest is this cash earning?

If I add up the dividends and the interest from my investments and cash, how much money will I have—on average—each month during my seventies?

Is that enough money to cover the monthly shortfall in my budget?

If it isn't, how can I change my budget? Is there anything I can reduce or eliminate from my budget and still have a good life?

If I can't cover my expenses using only the interest and dividend income, how can I *increase* the amount I take from my investments without "killing" the golden goose? In other words, what principal can I use for this decade that will not hurt me in the next decade?

You don't have to do this alone. Your financial professional can help you rearrange your investments to create enough income—enough golden eggs—from these investments without destroying the vital part of your principal—without killing the golden goose.

It's also a good time to meet with your financial professional because, based on current tax laws, you have to begin taking money out of your defined-contribution plan at the beginning of your seventies. You'll need to begin to withdraw a percentage of principal from your 401(k), 403(b), or SEP-IRA money. To make your life-planning work for this time frame and for the next, remember to not kill the golden goose. Even though the tax laws say that money has to be withdrawn from the retirement plan and taxes have to be paid on it, that doesn't mean you have to spend the money. If you choose, the principal can still be protected for the next time frame—with careful professional help.

Do I have enough money from my interest and dividends
to cover, on the average, my monthly budget shortfall?

If I don't, what will I do about it?

Your Life Has to Work, and It's Your Job to Make It Work

This is your life! It's your life, and you *have* to make it
work—in all aspects. Right now, you're making the money part
of your life work for this time frame—your seventies. Look
behind you, around you. No one else is standing in line to make
your life work for you. It has to work, and it's your job to make it
work. You must be willing to focus to make your life-plan work.
You must be willing to focus on what you can control—planning
your life. We all know we can't control outcomes. But you must
take responsibility for planning your life with the expectation
that your life will work. There are no other options.

What do I need to do to get a money plan in place? What
information do I still need?

To whom should I talk?

As you've heard so many times in this book, money is only
part of the planning. It's an important part, because you must
have money to have a roof over your head, good medical care,
and choices in your life. But you can have a lot of money and be
miserable. You can be unhappy and alone. You can be boring
and bored. You can be afraid of the future and frustrated in the
present. You can feel useless and unvalued. Money alone won't
fix this. But if you have a plan to make the money work, then
you can make the other parts work, too. Your goal, for your life,
is to make all of your life work well and feel good for you.

So, as in chapter 11 when you were planning for your
sixties, you will need to ask yourself some questions about the
decade of your seventies:

> When I'm in my seventies, where will I live? Will the
> place that I call home give me the most emotional
> satisfaction? Will I be able to afford to live there?
> Will that place support any physical needs that I may
> have? Will I feel safe in that place?

"I think it's time for me to move out of my home, Ruth," my
client Jean explained. "It makes me sad, but I'd rather move on
my own terms than wait until my children decide to move me."
Jane said the last part of that sentence with a determined voice.

"I haven't told my children, yet. But I've found a place I
think will be perfect. It's not too far from where I live now, and I
can walk to a few shops. There's also a bus line. It's awfully hard,
though," she continued with sadness, "all those years of history
in my house."

Jane's voice trailed off, and she sat quietly for a moment.
Then she said with a short laugh, "And all the stuff. Goodness
gracious! How am I going to get through all the stuff? And I have
to. I just don't want anyone to decide when I will move. I want to
decide when I will move and where."

> When I am in my seventies, whom will I want to live
> with? And why?
>
> Who else will I want to include in my life? What other
> relationships will I want in my life that will give me
> satisfaction? A sense of belonging? Safety?
>
> What will I include in my life that will stimulate my think-
> ing—that will keep my brain alive? Will I study a
> language? Do crossword puzzles? Belong to a book
> group?
>
> What is "play" to me? What will I include in my life that
> is just plain fun?
>
> What will I include in my life that will stimulate me emo-
> tionally? That will create pleasure? Anticipation?

> What will make me feel good about myself? Make me feel needed and valued? Loved and lovable?
>
> What will I do to take care of my physical body? What kind of exercise will I do to keep my body limber and healthy? What will my body need for nutrition? Where will I get support for taking care of my physical body?

"Guess what, Ruth? I'm taking a yoga class," Ann explained. "I'm seventy-five, and I just started this class with two other women—both younger than me. Actually, I'm the oldest one in the class. I don't have to drive. One of the women picks me up. You should see me stretch and bend," she continued with a chuckle. "It's really quite something."

> What will my volunteer work be—work that's not for income? How will I still be of service? How will I still know that I'm needed? What will I do so I know I'm adding back to the world—both to my world of family and friends and to the greater world?

"When it's not raining or it's not too cold," Madeline explained to me, "I walk the two blocks over to the elementary school and read to the first and second graders. Tuesday and Thursday mornings—that's when I go. It is such fun, and they do love it so. And," she added, "so do I."

> What will I do to create my legacy? What will determine how I want to be remembered, that my being here mattered?

Get clear. Stay creative. Be purposeful.

This is your life. Make it work—physically, emotionally, spiritually, and financially.

CHAPTER THIRTEEN

So, Is This Old?
Your Eighties and Older

It is not the length of life. It is the depth of life.
—Ralph Waldo Emerson

Welcome to your eighties! Most eighty- and ninety-year-olds would probably disagree with half of what Ralph Waldo Emerson said. As one eighty-two-year-old woman told me, "When people are forty or fifty years old, they say they would rather die than not have the highest quality of life. But when you get to my age, you want to live. You want to live and live well," she continued, "even with some compromises."

So maybe Ralph Waldo Emerson was in his forties or fifties when he wrote that statement. People in middle age don't want to think about getting old and dependent and having pain. They don't want to think about dying. So they say things like, "I'd rather die younger and have a better life while I'm alive." Or, "I have no interest in getting really old. I want to live as long as I can be independent and active."

Of course that's what you're going to say when you're forty! But when you're eighty you'll most likely think differently. Oh, when you're eighty, you may not be able to walk the stairs without knee pain—you may need a cane to help you. When you're eighty, you may look in the mirror some days and be startled by the face that looks back at you—old and wrinkly—when you don't feel old and wrinkly inside.

One day I received a call from an aunt who had just turned eighty and had cataract surgery on one of her eyes. Once that eye healed she was planning to get the other eye done. When I picked up the phone, she exclaimed, "Why didn't you tell me?"

"Tell you what?" I asked, puzzled.

"That I have wrinkles all over my face!" Obviously the bandage had been removed from her eye that day, and she had taken a good look at herself.

"I think you look great!" I said with absolute truth.

"I thought I looked pretty good for my age, too, until now," she replied. "But this is ridiculous! I look old!"

"Don't get the other eye done," I suggested.

"That's not funny, Ruth," she scolded me.

Then I told her the truth. "You are eighty years old. You've earned those wrinkles, if nothing else because you have me for a niece. You are smart, active, well read, well dressed, loving, and loved. You are financially independent and, for now, physically independent. You're wonderful and a great role model for my daughters and me. And you're still here and hopefully will be for a very long time!"

By the time you reach eighty, you may have needed to be very resilient and already have made many changes in your life-plan. But, even with those changes, you're still here and purposefully planning your life. You're still here and want to be here for a very long time.

Even if you aren't eighty years old, think of yourself as an eighty-year-old as you work through this chapter. Just like the last two chapters, this chapter will serve as a practice for you. It is important that you "try on" this stage, too, so that it feels real to you. Practicing being in your eighties, even if you're not, will help you plan more effectively for this decade of your life.

So let's start that planning.

A Clear Vision Reprograms Your Brain with *Your* Picture of *Your* Life, Not a Picture of Someone Else's Life

In this time frame—your eighties—like the previous time frames, planning has to start with a clear vision. You already know the importance of a vision statement in creating a purposeful plan. A vision statement creates a picture of what you want your life to look like and feel like and what you want to experience. Without this picture, the only "vision" your brain has is a picture of eighty based on what you have "seen" by experience. In other words, your brain's only picture is what was imprinted on it by whatever you saw in your life from other people who were eighty, what they looked liked at eighty or older, what they said about being eighty or older, what choices they had in their lives during their eighties. That is your picture if you haven't revised your brain's predetermined mindset about being eighty and older. If you want something different for your eighties, you'll need to create a new picture.

My vision for my eighties is: "I will continue to hike to whatever ability I have, sharing these experiences with my partner for as long as we have together. This may be the decade to downsize the family home and move to something with less maintenance. I will stay near family and friends—my community— even though we may spend a couple of months a year in a different location. My volunteer life will be strong. I will find the time to work on my mystery book—probably the same one I started in my seventies. I will still be feisty and, by now, may need a separate closet for all my big hats."

What is my vision for my eighties and beyond? What do I want to create spiritually, emotionally, physically, and financially? What do I want my eighties and beyond to look like and feel like?

Write down your vision statement for your eighties.

So, with your vision—your picture—in mind, let's get specific.

One of the differences between this decade and the past two decades is that money isn't the primary worry. Independence and physical care take priority for most men and women eighty and older. Eighty-year-olds are concerned about how long they can remain independent. They're worried about how they'll take care of themselves, especially if something bad happens like a serious fall or an illness. They're worried about who will help them if they need help. *Then* they get to the money facet—they worry about how they'll pay for the care they'll need.

At eighty and beyond, you have to be able to afford the cost of taking care of yourself spiritually, emotionally, and physically. So even though money appears to be secondary for most eighty-year-olds, let's deal with money first.

Your Golden Goose Will Now Take Care of You

First, congratulate yourself for financially taking care of yourself so well in your sixties and seventies—the first two time frames in stage three of your life. In those first two time frames, you purposefully planned your finances so you wouldn't use the principal of your money. You purposefully didn't kill your golden goose. You saved your principal for this time frame, when you are the most vulnerable financially. Most men and women in their eighties are not earning significant—if any—income. Because of that, they are more dependent on their accumulated money. Most men and women in their eighties have increased health care costs, which can create a financial burden. And since, as you already know, health care costs have a higher inflationary rate than most other areas of consumer spending, the financial burden of health care is likely to increase during the eighties and beyond.

So what's the financial strategy for this decade and the next? Spend your money! Now that's not quite as frivolous a piece of advice as it sounds. But the bottom line is, this is the time frame to use your principal. And use it purposefully.

Purposefully plan for this decade financially, just as you did in your sixties and seventies.

What Are My Expenses?

Let's work with expenses first. How much will you need to pay your bills and expenses when you're eighty and older? To calculate this figure for the third time frame in stage three, use the same structure as in the last two chapters.

What you're looking for is the total amount of money you'll need each month to pay your expenses and bills and your taxes and benefits. You may want to go back to chapter 12 to answer the question, "What are my expenses?" Then, to bring this number up-to-date for this time frame, ask yourself:

At eighty and older, will any of the expenses or bills that are *now* a part of my life be gone?

What are these expenses?

What is the total amount of these expenses?

Now, calculate the total amount of money you'll need in your eighties and beyond using the budget amount from chapter 12.

Subtract—Expenses that will *not* be part of my life during this decade.

What is that number?

Now, ask yourself:

As an eighty-year-old, do I have any *new* or *increased* expenses or bills in my life that are not part of my life *right now*?

What are the *new* or *increased* expenses that need to be added?

What is the total cost of these *new* or *increased* expenses?

Now, add this number to the calculation you just did when you subtracted expenses from your budget for your seventies.

What is that new budgeting number? As in chapter 12, this amount doesn't include income taxes. Income taxes still have to be paid on the retirement income you have even if you have little or no earned income. There are a few exceptions to this, so check with your financial professional. To determine how much money you'll need to pay your income taxes, get help from your financial professional, who can also help you factor in inflation. Also—just a reminder—make sure you plan for probable higher health care costs.

How much money, including taxes, do I need each month to pay my bills and expenses during my eighties and beyond?

Add to this total the amount you've already figured to pay for benefits. At this age your health care policy and your long-term care policy *must* be maintained. Be sure the premiums for these insurances are paid when they're due. One possibility is to have them paid automatically from your checking account so you don't overlook them.

What is the total—including bills and expenses, taxes and benefits—that I'll need for my bills and expenses in my eighties and beyond?

What Are My Sources of Income?

Now that you've figured out how much your life costs you, determine how much money you *know* you'll have. This is money that comes in regularly each month.

Will I still be earning any money—even if it's small—each month?

Can you count on this money each month? If not, you may not want to include it.

What is the total amount of money I receive each month from regular sources—my Social Security, my defined-benefit retirement income, and any annuity income.

Now, subtract this income amount from the amount of my monthly expenses.

What amount of my monthly expenses are not covered by the income I receive from regular sources? In other words, how much is my monthly shortfall?

This shortfall is the amount of money you'll need to take out of your defined-contribution investments—your 401(k), 403(b), SEP IRA, or SIMPLE. It will also include any other money that you have kept invested for this time frame which could include your Roth IRA investment if you have one. Your financial professional will help you decide which investments to sell to pay for this shortfall and which investments to continue to hold. Get expert planning help so you know your money will last as long as you do. You may live longer than you planned. Now that's a nice thought!

So, congratulations! All of your planning is paying off. You're still here. That's good. And so is your money. That's good, too. Your strategy to preserve your principal through your sixties and seventies has paid off. Now you have the money to take care of yourself without worry. There's an old saying in the financial community: "You have planned well the use of your money and how long it needs to last if you have enough money before you die, but the check that your relatives write to the funeral home bounces." Now, that may in reality be cutting it a bit close. But you get the idea—spend your money to take care of yourself in the next decade or two (your eighties and nineties). Be happy. Be safe. Don't worry. That's why you have been so purposefully planning during these decades.

But as you've heard so many times in this book, planning your money life, as important as it is, isn't enough. You need to make the other parts of your life work too. As in your sixties and seventies, your goal is to make all of your life work well and feel good.

Life-Planning Involves More Than Money

As in chapter 11, when you planned for your sixties, and in chapter 12, when you planned for your seventies, when planning for your eighties and beyond, you need to ask yourself a few questions. Some of these questions may be difficult to think about. Maybe it's difficult to think of yourself as an eighty- or ninety-year-old. Maybe this age creates fear in you. If that happens, go back and reread your vision statement for this time frame. Rework it if necessary so you can picture yourself in this time frame—making your life work.

When I'm in my eighties, where will I live? Will the place I call home give me the most emotional satisfaction? Will I be able to afford to live there? Will that place support any physical needs I may have? Will I feel safe in that place?

When I'm in my eighties, whom do I want to live with? And why?

Who else will I want to include in my life? What other relationships will give me satisfaction? A sense of belonging? A sense of safety?

What will I include in my life to stimulate me emotionally? To create pleasure in my life? Anticipation? To make me feel happy and good about myself? To make me feel needed and valued? Loved and lovable?

When you're eighty—and eighty-six and ninety-two—you still need to think about what excites you and creates anticipation for you. You'll want to continue to try new things to keep your emotions alive and stimulated.

A couple of years ago, I attended a banquet where I was to receive an award for my professional work. There were about 800 people there and, as numerous people were congratulating me before the dinner, something caught my attention out of the corner of my eye. I turned around and there stood my diminutive, ninety-four-year-old aunt. I was astounded. Her health was fragile—particularly her heart—and I couldn't believe she would risk her health just to be part of the celebration. With tears in my eyes, I gave her a hug and said, "I can't believe you're here. I'll never forget that you came."

With a big grin on her face, she interrupted me as she exclaimed, "*You* won't forget I'm here? What about *me?* I'm here, Ruth! I'll never forget that I'm really here. Wouldn't miss it for the world!"

So try new things. Go to new places. My aunt has trouble with her hearing and doesn't see well. This didn't bother her at the banquet—or anyone else—and she had a wonderful time. Try new things that make you anticipate doing them, things that make you excited when you relive them. My aunt called me several days after the banquet and said, "Didn't we have fun? Don't wait too long to get another award," she continued, "because I am ninety-four years old, you know, and I want to be there."

What will I include in my life to stimulate my thinking— to keep my brain alive? Will I study a language? Do crossword puzzles? Belong to a book group? Watch travel videos?

You may be wondering where that travel video question came from. An older couple I know used to travel a great deal until their late seventies. They had to stop because of physical limitations, so now, in their mid-eighties, they rent a travel video most Sunday afternoons. They make popcorn and take a trip from the comfort of their living room.

What will I do to take care of my physical body? What kind of exercise will keep my body limber and healthy? What will my body need for nutrition? Where will I get support for taking care of my physical body? Are my doctors paying attention? Respecting my needs?

How will I still be of service? To my family? To my religious community? Or to the greater world? How will I know that I'm still needed? Valued? That I still have a contribution to make?

Is my planning for my legacy in place? Have I determined how I want to be remembered? How do I know that my being here really and truly mattered?

Again, as in the last two chapters, be clear.
Stay creative. Be purposeful.
This is your life. You are purposefully making it work.

CHAPTER FOURTEEN

What About Now?

Today is the first day of the rest of your life.
—Charles Dederrich

The other day my daughter and I took a shopping trip to the Mall of America. Yes! I mean *the* Mall of America. It's the largest indoor shopping center in the world, and it really is a monstrosity of a building. We entered the building through one of the main doors and just stood there, trying to decide which way to go. Then I saw a kiosk with a map of the mall. On the map I saw a little red dot that said, "You are here." From where we were we could figure out how to get to the shops of our choice. We didn't feel confused or uncertain anymore. We knew where we were going and how to get there. We had a plan.

This final chapter is rather like that kiosk at the Mall of America. Here we have this wonderful monstrosity called your life. It's huge, possibly ninety or more years! On the map of your life, where are you now? Are you twenty-three—the end of stage one? Are you thirty-three—the beginning of stage two? Are you forty-two—in stage two of your life? Or fifty-six—still in stage two? Or are you seventy—in stage three?

Where are you today?

Look at all you've worked through in this book:

You've practiced the skill of managing your emotions.

You've learned about healthy defiance.

You are learning the skill of resiliency.

You've learned about yourself as a person—what you like and don't like.

You've learned about your work—your work for pay and work not for pay—and what feeds you and what drains you about your work.

You've learned about the principles of money and how to apply them to your life.

You've created a vision for all three time frames of stage three—normally called retirement. This vision has helped you see a new way to live and live purposefully for the last third of your life.

Congratulations! You've done good work.

Today Is a Beginning

But now it's today. You don't need to wait until you're sixty to take purposeful control of your life. **Start where you are!** Today is a beginning. What you do or don't do *today* directly affects what happens to you when you're sixty and seventy and eighty. Remember, all the stages of your life are unique and all the stages are interrelated. What you do or don't do today will determine the success of your next stage and choices you have in the next stage. So, no matter what stage you're in and what time frame in that stage, *today* is the day to start purposefully planning for the last stage of your life. You know that there are no guarantees for the future, but knowing that there are no guarantees does *not* take away your personal responsibility for purposefully taking charge of your life. It is your responsibility for planning your life—in the present and for the future.

Purposeful planning always starts with a vision. You need to form a vision—a picture—of your life in the time frame you are in—right now.

Ask yourself:

What is my vision for where I am in my life right now?

Since all the stages of my life are interrelated, how will my present-day vision contribute to the life-planning success of the next stage?

"I know I've been in the midlife doldrums, Ruth" my client Tim explained. "Working hard. Not getting ahead. Not getting behind either. And nothing bad really happening, just the same old same old every day. I just couldn't see any further than the next work day and the next bill to pay. But, Ruth, you know, I get it now," his voice carried a bit of excitement. "This is just one part of my life. And it feeds the next part. I know this probably sounds kind of silly to you, but seeing the bigger picture and how all of this ties together really helps me. When I go to the club in the morning before work, I'm taking care of myself now and for the future. When I put my money into my 401(k)—rather than bemoaning the fact that I could use that money today to pay bills—I'm doing what I need to now to take care of the future. When Jan and I take the time to go for a walk or see a movie, we're not just grabbing a little time, we're keeping our relationship strong so we have a good relationship now *and* in the future. Seeing the big picture and seeing how it ties into today really helps, Ruth. It really helps."

So start where you are. Think about how you can make your present-day life work in such a way that will give you more choices for the next stage. Be sure to take into consideration the four facets of a balanced life. These four facets are, as you already know, spiritual, emotional, physical, and financial.

Ask yourself:

How do I define spirituality?

How does my life reflect my spirituality—today?

What do I need to do to increase the sense of my own spirituality—today?

Am I willing to actually do what I need to do?

How do I define emotional health?

How does my life reflect my emotional health—today?

What do I need to do to increase the sense of my own emotional health—today?

Am I willing to actually do what I need to do?

How do I define physical health?

How does my life reflect my physical health—today?

What do I need to do to increase the sense of my own physical health—today?

Am I willing to actually do what I need to do?

How do I define financial health?

How does my life reflect my financial health—today?

What do I need to do to increase the sense of my own financial health—today?

Am I willing to actually do what I need to do?

Your future really does start today. It's so important that you take ownership of your life—spiritually, emotionally, physically, and financially.

Take care of yourself and your relationships—today. If you are unhappy and can't get out of the doldrums, get help. I believe in experts. Find an emotional expert—a therapist—if you need one. Find a spiritual expert—a spiritual counselor or a religious leader—to help you sort through your life and what you need to be healthy emotionally and spiritually. Smart people ask for help. Smart people know they can't fix everything themselves. Smart people value themselves and their lives and create the change that's necessary for health.

Take care of your work. If your work makes you miserable, make an appointment with a vocational or career counselor and figure out what work you can do to get some degree of satisfaction—and still get paid enough money. For your life-planning to be successful, you need to find meaningful work now. Don't wait. Get help if you need it.

Take care of your body. Remember your body is the vehicle in which you travel through life. If you don't have a healthily functioning body, it's harder to get through life. Buy a treadmill—and use it. Join a health club—and go. Schedule time to take care of your physical body. See your dentist. Keep your doctors' appointments. Think prevention—not crisis.

Take care of your money. The closer you follow the principles of money (chapter 9), the more successful you will be. The earlier you start to practice the principles of money, the more choices you'll have in the next stages of your life. If you haven't been able to accumulate money for stage three, today is the day to start. Don't wait. Lower your expenses. Find a way to increase your income. Do something—today. Put away even a small amount each payday—and leave it there. You have to. It's your life, and it's your responsibility to make your life work—all of it.

Every day, in my office, I listen to the regrets that wonderful people like you have about their lives. Every day. I listen to the "If only . . ." and the "I should haves. . . ." I hear the pain. I hear the frustration. I hear the discouragement. I have also noted that the older the person, the greater the discouragement. Older stage two people are more frustrated than late stage one people. Stage three people are the most frustrated and have the most regrets. "If only I had understood how important time was." Or, "How did I get so caught up in my work that I didn't plan for the future?" One man said to me, "Did I think I was going to die at sixty-two? What was the matter with me? Why didn't I find a way to put away more money?"

These are regrets. Regrets are emotional responses to loss. We feel regret when we haven't fulfilled our desires or done the things we wanted to do. We feel loss for opportunities that are gone.

Ask yourself:

How would I express a regret I have—right now?

If I *don't* take the actions—spiritually, emotionally, physically, financially—that I know I need to take, what regrets do I think I'll have *ten years* from now? *Twenty years* from now? *Thirty years* from now?

What can I do *today* that will lessen those regrets? What information do I need? What actions do I need to take?

When you're willing to do what's needed to make your life work, you'll have fewer regrets as you go through the stages of your life. You now have information to do what you need to do.

You now understand the importance of managing your emotions and being resilient.

You now have vision statements for all the stages of your life.

You understand yourself and what's important to you.

You understand the role that work has in your life.

You understand the principles of money and how essential they are to making your life work.

You have a new way to see the stages of your life and how all the stages interconnect—especially with the last stage of your life.

You have a process now to purposefully plan for the last twenty-five to thirty-five years of your life, a process that will enhance the quality of your whole life—spiritually, emotionally, physically and of course, financially.

So, **start where you are**, now! Make your life work. You'll never regret it.